CIVIL WAR CHRONICLES
NAVAL WARFARE

Tom Freeman
© 1993

CIVIL WAR CHRONICLES

NAVAL WARFARE

COURAGE AND COMBAT ON THE WATER

JOHN C. WIDEMAN

MetroBooks

An Imprint of Friedman/Fairfax Publishers

Library of Congress Cataloging-in-Publication Data

Wideman, John C.
       Naval warfare: courage and combat on the water / John Wideman.
          p.   cm. — (Civil War chronicles)
       Includes bibliographical references and index.
       ISBN 1-56799-425-5
       1. United States—History—Civil War, 1861-1865—Naval operations.
  I. Series: Civil War chronicles (MetroBooks (Firm))
  E591.W38   1997
  973.7'5—DC20   96-34370

Consulting Editor: David Phillips
Editor: Tony Burgess
Art Director: Kevin Ullrich
Designer: Garrett Schuh
Photography Editor: Kathryn Culley
Production Manager: Camille Lee

Color separations by Bright Arts Graphics Pte. Ltd.
Printed in China by Leefung-Asco Printers Ltd.

10 9 8 7 6 5 4 3 2 1

For bulk purchases and special sales, please contact:
Friedman/Fairfax Publishers
Attention: Sales Department
15 West 26th Street
New York, NY 10010
(212) 685-6610 FAX (212) 685-1307

Visit our website:
http://www.metrobooks.com

DEDICATION

To BM1 John C. Wideman, Sr. (USN 1941–1945), my father and
an iron man in wooden PT boats.

ACKNOWLEDGMENTS

No work is accomplished alone. In the course of its writing, several people contributed greatly to this book. STG1 Jeffrey L. Kelley (USN 1979–1992), my friend and colleague who proved to me the new navy is just as good as the "old" navy. My close friend, Dixon Ericson, who, as always, was my harshest critic and my guiding light. Tony Burgess, Kathryn Culley, and the other staff members of the Michael Friedman Publishing Group made all of this possible through their careful work, editing, and counseling.

CONTENTS

FOREWORD

Both the United States and the Confederate States faced enormous difficulties at the outset of the American Civil War, and these problems can be seen most clearly by comparing the state of their respective navies. The Confederacy had less than 250 naval officers available for duty, officers who had recently resigned National commissions in order to support their individual states. Other than a few small vessels confiscated from the Federal navy, the South possessed no actual fighting fleet.

Numerically, the North was better off, but most of its fleet was composed of older, obsolete ships. Furthermore, much of the North's naval strength was far from the coast of the United States, participating in the normal peacetime mission of protecting American interests at sea. The men in both navies had little experience or training to prepare them for the war that was developing. Any fighting experience that they did have involved combat at sea, against other ships in deep water. But in this new war, the men would be called upon to fight on rivers and within coastal areas in close coordina-tion with land forces, against armies and fortresses as well as enemy vessels.

Both the North and the South depended upon sea commerce. In the North, a great deal of money had been invested to develop a maritime industry that was second only to that of Great Britain. The merchant ships and whaling vessels of the Union sailed far and wide on all of the earth's oceans. The North was soon to discover, however, that these vessels were highly vulnerable to the depre-dations of even the few commerce raiders that managed to dart past Union vessels blockading Southern ports.

The new Confederacy was also highly dependent on maritime lines of communica-tion. Lacking indigenous industry sufficient to support a war economy, the agricultural South was highly dependent on imported manufactured items from prewar trading partners in Europe. The import of manufac-tured goods from Europe and the export of cotton to pay for them required unrestricted movement of ships across the Atlantic.

Recognizing these twin vulnerabilities at an early point, the Federal government real-ized that it could attempt to protect its own commerce from raiders while restricting the life-sustaining international trade from Southern ports through the use of a large-scale naval blockade. At the outbreak of hos-tilities, the Union government ordered its naval forces to positions offshore from the South's major ports. A significant vulnerabili-ty of the South had been identified, and sig-nificant Union maritime resources would be maintained against it for the remainder of the Civil War. The potential of the South's naval raiders to do significant damage to the Northern merchant fleet was reduced (but not eliminated) by this attempt to bottle up the Confederate navy in its ports, while the same strategy would reduce the ability of the resource-poor South to import vital military and civilian items from Europe and restrict the sale of cotton to raise war funds.

Another aspect of Federal naval strategy consisted of the use of highly mobile forces to move troops and heavy guns along major rivers to penetrate deeply into the interior of the Confederacy. Through the use of relative-ly fast river boats, the Union Army was able to move fresh troops along to reinforce fight-ing troops, rather than marching them from place to place. The new mobile river-borne strategy was soon to prove itself successful against forts Henry and Donelson, where generals Grant and Foote were able to force a successful entry of Federal forces into Tennessee, and effectively take Kentucky entirely out of the Civil War, as far as its Confederate sympathizers were concerned.

New strategies were combined with new weapons of war. Naval combat in the Civil War was to witness the first widespread use of armored warships, which at the time were little more than mobile platforms designed to transport heavy guns from one point to another. These new warships, including the Federal monitor-class ironclads, would engage in battles that would forever

A sleek Confederate blockade-runner slips out to sea, pursued by a Union cruiser on blockade duty.

change the nature of naval warfare, and that would be as important to the outcome of the war as the land battles.

The role of naval operations in the Civil War has not generally received the attention it deserves. With the present volume, John Wideman goes a long way toward correcting this shortcoming. He has brought together a wealth of information that makes it possible to fully evaluate the central importance of naval warfare to the outcome of the Civil War, a conflict whose effects continue to profoundly influence the political and social history of North America and, indeed, the world. As one of the United States' greatest military strategists, Alfred Thayer Mahan, wrote:

> "... *Never did sea power play a greater or more decisive part than in the contest which determined that the course of world history would be modified by the existence of one great nation, instead of several rival states, on the North American continent.*"

—David Phillips

INTRODUCTION

"Except its officers, the Confederate government had nothing in the shape of a navy. It had not a single ship-of-war."

—Professor Soley, quoted by J. Thomas Scharf in History of the Confederate States Navy

THE U.S. NAVY AT THE WAR'S BEGINNING

At the beginning of the Civil War, Gideon Welles was appointed by President Abraham Lincoln as Secretary of the United States Navy. The secession of the Southern states was rapid, and Welles was caught unprepared for war. The U.S. Navy (a fleet of fewer than sixty ships) had begun extending its global influence after the War of 1812, and had twenty-eight of its ships located on foreign duty all around the world. Approximately twenty percent of the officers in the U.S. Navy resigned their commissions and offered their services to their native Southern states, and subsequently to the Confederacy. Welles had too few ships, too few officers and men, and too much enemy coastline (about thirty-five hundred miles [5600km]) to control.

President Abraham Lincoln declared a blockade of the South, which had one unintended and undesirable consequence: under international law, this gave the South status as a legitimate belligerent. Had he instead declared that the U.S. Navy was closing the ports of the southern coast in order to suppress an internal insurrection, the Confederacy would not have been able to deal with other nations as an independent warring party.

When the war began in April 1861, Welles had only eight vessels of the Home Squadron immediately available for use, and only four of these were steamers. The rest of the fleet was in foreign waters or laid up in various naval yards and unavailable for duty. By December 1861, however, the industrial

might of the North had begun to overcome many of its equipment problems. The U.S. Navy by then consisted of 264 vessels armed with 2,557 guns and manned by twenty-five thousand naval personnel.

Welles began buying up all nature of commercial vessels and converting them for military service. Virtually anything that would float was pressed into service as a blockader. In 1861 alone, 136 vessels were purchased and converted to warships. For instance, the USS *Commodore Perry*, a New York ferryboat, was converted to carry four 9-inch (22.8cm) smoothbore cannon, a 12-pounder (5.4kg) rifle, and a 100-pounder (45.4kg) rifle. The *Commodore Perry* and the rest of the ragtag flotilla was organized and steamed south in early 1862 under the command of Admiral L.M. Goldsborough to seal off portions of the North Carolina coast, a task for which it was hardly prepared.

U.S. NAVY ORGANIZATION

The Union naval officer command structure was composed of regulars and volunteers. Regular naval officers were career navy line officers, nearly all of whom were graduates of the U.S. Naval Academy at Annapolis, Maryland. When war began, Welles ordered the top three classes of midshipmen at the Naval Academy to active duty as officers in the U.S. Navy. Volunteer officers were mostly merchant vessel captains from the North's great mercantile fleet.

Enlisted men in the U.S. Navy were both regular and volunteers. Initially, there were not enough men to service the ships required for all the naval operations. Various enlistment gimmicks were used to entice men to sea. But the navy wound up taking just about anyone who would agree to serve. As early as 1861, former slaves, foreign sea-

Gideon Welles, the iron-willed Connecticut Yankee, was chosen by Lincoln to head the ill-prepared U.S. Navy. Welles, a shrewd politician, put his personal attributes to great use and formed the navy into a world-class sea force.

men, and any others willing to serve were enlisted. As the war progressed and more ships came on line, army units were discharged in large groups to become navy personnel.

Welles organized the navy into squadrons and flotillas. There were essentially six main squadrons during the war: the North Atlantic Squadron (responsible for the Virginia and North Carolina coasts), the South Atlantic Squadron (responsible for South Carolina, Georgia, and Florida's Atlantic coast), the East Gulf Squadron (responsible for all of Florida's west coast), the West Gulf Squadron (responsible for all coastline from Florida to Mexico), the Mississippi River Squadron (responsible for the Mississippi River and all its tributaries down to New Orleans), and the Pacific Squadron, which saw little action. Flotillas

PAGE 11: At the war's beginning, the Union rushed to reinforce critical coastal garrisons. Here, Union troops land at Fort Pickens, on Florida's panhandle, in June 1861. The troop ship has no metal armor or protection; naval warriors had not yet learned the importance of such defenses. ABOVE: The waist-length "shell jacket" worn by U.S. Navy enlisted personnel. It was usually reserved for formal occasions, as combat crewmen preferred a pullover sweater that was also issued.

were detachments broken off from squadrons for temporary duty. For example, the Mississippi Flotilla served in the assaults on forts Henry and Donelson and returned to be part of the Mississippi Squadron after that action had been concluded.

THE CONFEDERATE NAVY AT THE WAR'S BEGINNING

Secretary of the Navy Stephen R. Mallory, Confederate States of America, had a different problem from that of Welles in 1861. Mallory had no navy whatsoever, and each state was raising its military forces with no coordination with the central government or the other states. Confederate Navy officers came from resignations in the U.S. Navy and from commercial ship captains. Mallory established a naval academy at Richmond, Virginia, and by the end of 1861 the Confederate Navy had taken form. It had at least thirty-four vessels and eighty-seven officers.

Mallory istill lacked ships, however, and he immediately began an ambitious plan to build a navy from scratch. His initial plan involved the construction of ironclad ships to break the blockade, and the construction of raiders to interdict U.S. commerce on the high seas. Mallory's initial fleet came mostly from seizures of U.S. ships. Several ships, most notably the *Merrimack,* were salvaged in whole or in part from the Union's failure to totally destroy them at their respective Union navy yards. Several U.S. Navy ships were seized in southern harbors. Other ships were converted, as in the North, from commercial ships.

This cutaway view of an early American man-of-war shows the placement of personnel and stores in the decks below the gun decks. Ships like this one operated mostly in the open sea; the deep draft of their keels made them unsuitable for shallow waters.

Stephen Mallory, Gideon Welles' opposite number in the Confederacy, was a maritime lawyer from Key West and one of Florida's senators before the war. As the chairman of the Senate's Naval Affairs Committee, he gained experience and knowledge that would prove invaluable when he faced the task of building the Confederate Navy from scratch.

The Confederate Navy invented naval mines (called "torpedoes" at the time) and used them in ingenious ways to deny Union ships access to critical ports and channel them into areas where they could be brought under coastal battery fire. These mines are metal canisters filled with powder, floated by empty wooden casks, and fired by electrical fuses.

Mallory, through an intermediary, began making secret arrangements with shipbuilders in England to construct a number of first-class cruisers for use by the Confederate Navy in combat against Union warships and commercial craft. A number of ships were built and delivered to the Confederacy. England came to regret the contract when, after the war, an international court of claims ordered England to pay the United States of America $15.5 million in gold to compensate for damage done by commerce raiders built in England.

Mallory, as former Chairman of the U.S. Senate Committee on Naval Affairs, realized early on the necessity for ironclad ships. In addition to the English-built commerce raiders, he ordered the domestic construction of ironclads, including the former USS *Merrimack,* fated to become the CSS *Virginia.* Ironclad construction began at the various Confederate naval yards throughout the South. By June 1861, Mallory had naval engineers working on construction plans for an ironclad to be built on the hull of the salvaged *Merrimack.*

NAVAL WARFARE IN THE MID–NINETEENTH CENTURY

Understanding any military endeavor, naval or otherwise, must begin with a knowledge of the weapons and tactics used by all participants. Men in ships do not just sail up to each other and fire away with whatever is at hand. Warfare evolves by invention and research—and sometimes by sheer accident. The American Civil War was no exception to this rule.

For naval purposes, America's most recent serious conflict had been the War of 1812. Although the U.S. Navy conducted extensive scientific experimentation in the 1840s and 1850s, by 1861, most, if not all, of the naval personnel who had combat experience were dead or retired. On the eve of the Civil War, therefore, the U.S. Navy, although made up of professionals, was almost entirely untried in combat. American military personnel watched the various European conflicts of the first half of the nineteenth century (e.g. the Napoleonic Wars, the Crimean War) with interest. European tactical doctrines

Since almost everything aboard a naval man-of-war had to be made or repaired aboard ship, a crew usually included artisans such as carpenters, ironmengers, and millwrights. These sailors (called "jack-tars" in the old navy) are posed with their work tools on the deck of a warship.

were in vogue in the various American military academies.

Prior to Robert Fulton's application of the steam engine to watercraft, ships moved by the grace of God and the elements. Wind propelled navies to their rendezvous. Sea battles were won and lost with the vagaries of wind and tide. By 1861, however, the steam engine was in common use as motive power (usually in combination with sails) on many boats in inland waters and on the high seas. Steam power propelled a ship through the use of a screw (propeller) or a paddle wheel. Screws were the more efficient of the propulsion methods, and were used extensively on deepwater vessels.

Naval Artillery and Armor

Naval artillery in use during the Civil War consisted of two main types of muzzle-loading guns: smoothbore and rifled. As the name suggests, smoothbore artillery was simply a smooth tube, usually made from bronze or reinforced iron, which fired a round ball. A rifled gun, however, had

The 32-pounder bow rifle on the Teaser, a 64-ton (57.6t.) wooden-hulled tug that was originally in the Confederate Navy, armed with a 2.9-inch (7.4cm) Parrot rifle. Captured by the USS Maratanza in July 1862, it served ably in Virginia rivers until the war's end. Note the shell sitting on the rail: it has two bands, of either wrought copper or lead, that engaged the rifling in the barrel and gave spin, and therefore stability, to the projectile.

grooves, or rifling, in the barrel, and fired an elongated shell. Rifles had several advantages over smoothbore cannon by virtue of the spin imparted to the projectile by the rifling. Rifles had longer ranges and better accuracy, and maintained more of their inertia (or "punch") at greater ranges and, therefore, penetrated better. On the downside, rifles were somewhat harder to load, required specialized ammunition, and took longer to fire than smoothbores.

Naval guns today are identified according to the diameter of their barrels, measured in millimeters, but in the nineteenth century they were designated either according to the weight of their projectile or according to their diameter measured in inches. Thus, a "32-pounder" was a gun that hurled a thirty-two-pound (14.5kg) spherical iron ball from its muzzle, while a "10-inch" gun fired a projectile ten inches (25.4cm) in diameter.

There were several different types of projectiles in use aboard ship during the Civil War. Round shot (also called solid shot) was a solid round or elongated iron ball that was used as a battering projectile. It was fired against land-based forts to knock down walls and at other ships to tear away rigging and sunder wooden planking.

Explosive shells (sometimes referred to as bombs) were hollow, cast-iron spheres filled with black powder. At one point on the shell's surface, a hole was drilled into the sphere to accept a fuse device. When the shell was fired, the fuse was lit, or actuated, by the propelling explosion. When the fuse burned down, the shell exploded, sending shards of the cast-iron casing in every direction. In theory, the fuse burned at a known rate and the gunner, knowing the velocity of his round and the length of the fuse, could time a projectile to explode at a given point. This was rarely true in practice because of the inconsistency of the manufacture of the fuse and the effects of humidity and age on

the explosive contents. Shells were fired at other ships and at troops in the open. The exploding shells destroyed rigging and injured exposed personnel. Obviously, a significant amount of cover could render the shell ineffective. To this end, most forts of the era contained "bomb-proof" shelters.

Antipersonnel rounds come in three varieties: canister (sometimes called "case shot"), grapeshot, and spherical case shot. Canister was simply a can filled with lead balls. When fired, the balls left the can much in the way buckshot leaves the muzzle of a modern shotgun. The spreading balls cut down troops in the open. It was not very effective against covered troops.

Grape shot was a group of iron balls on a wooden stand covered with a cloth bag.

Each group of balls was separated horizontally from the other by a metal disk. In the center of the balls was a wooden dowel holding the whole thing together. When fired from a gun, the bag disintegrated and the balls flew about like common buckshot. This round was very effective against troops in the open and could be put to good use destroying the rigging of a ship.

Spherical case shot was a combination of a fused case shot, or bomb, filled with iron balls and powder. Spherical case shot was sometimes called shrapnel, after a similar invention by a British officer early in the nineteenth century. Upon being fired, the fuse was lit by the propelling charge and, down range, the round exploded, sending the case fragments and the iron balls flying

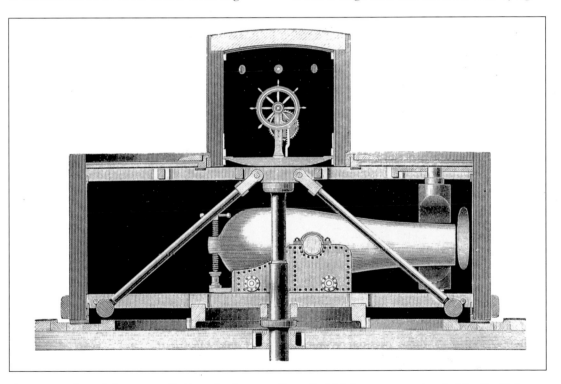

A cutaway view of the turret of a Passaic-class monitor, of which ten were constructed for the Union Navy. Designed by the Swedish naval genius John Ericsson, they were the first iron ships to be built in quantity. The gun shown is a smoothbore cannon. Each Passaic-class monitor had one 15-inch (38.1cm) smoothbore and one 11-inch (27.9 cm) smoothbore, side by side in the turret. The room above the guns is the pilothouse, where the captain and the pilot controlled the ship in combat, sending messages to the engineroom by signals and a speaking tube.

Experienced "jack-tars" of the U.S. Navy aboard the USS Wissahickon, posed next to an 11-inch (27.9cm) Dahlgren smoothbore cannon on a pivot mount. One of twenty-three Unadilla-class wooden, two-masted schooner gunboats, the Wissahickon was built in forty-five days from green, unseasoned wood. It served throughout the entire war, from the Mississippi River to the Atlantic coast. The single pivot gun was set up on rails so that it could be adjusted to fire in any direction.

*This painting by William R. McGrath shows an underwater view of the CSS **Hunley** as she detonates her spar torpedo against the hull of the USS **Housatonic** in Charleston harbor.*

in every direction. This was used against unprotected troops and sailors on deck.

One other type of projectile deserves mention: the carcass. The carcass was a hollow iron ball filled with pitch and chemicals. The case had holes in it. When fired, the pitch and chemicals would ignite and burn for about eight minutes. Carcasses were fired against wooden ships, powder magazines, and other highly flammable objects.

The Confederate Navy also developed innovative weapons that marked the beginnings of undersea warfare. Spar torpedoes were explosive charges placed at the end of a long pole, or spar. They either were fitted with a contact fuse, which exploded on contact with the side of a ship, or were command-detonated by one of the crew once contact had been made. Spar torpedoes were fitted to small cutters, sometimes called "Davids" after the first spar torpedo boat, the CSS *David*. In addition, the Confederate Navy developed one of the first operational sub-

marines, the CSS *Hunley*. First placed in service in August 1863, the *Hunley* promptly sank at her moorings. Undaunted, the Confederate submariners raised her from the muck of Charleston harbor and recommissioned her. During a trial run in October 1863, she sank with all hands, killing nine sailors. She was raised and recommissioned again. On February 17, 1864, the *Hunley* crept up on the USS *Housatonic,* anchored in Charleston harbor. She ran her spar topedo against the *Housatonic's* hull, blowing a gaping hole below the waterline and sinking her. Unfortunately, the *Hunley* and her entire crew were also lost during the engagement.

In the early stages of the war, much attention was given to the problem of protecting ships against both naval artillery and ground artillery. French successes using ironclad vessels (notably the *Gloire* in the war against Russia), the destruction of the Turkish wooden fleet by the Russians at Sinope, and the British development of the all-metal war-

ship *Warrior* inspired a change in technology. Military engineers began research and development on armor plating for ships and on weapons capable of penetrating that armor. The generally accepted formula in the mid-nineteenth century was that a fortified land-based gun was equal to five ship-mounted guns on a wooden ship.

Most armor consisted of iron plate, iron railroad rails, or iron bars affixed to a heavy backing of timber. The iron was placed in horizontal and vertical layers over a thick oak superstructure. The iron was usually four to eight inches (10.2–20.3cm) thick, and the wood was usually at least two feet (0.6m) thick. The Confederate ironclads and the Union river ironclads were similarly constructed. Both sides supplemented armor plate with the use of cotton bales, timber, and even chains linked together. (The exception was the series of Union armored vessels of the *Monitor* design, discussed in detail in a later chapter.)

The most vulnerable points on a ship are its motive power plant system, waterline, and steering mechanism. Without power or the ability to steer, a ship simply sits dead in the water and is shot to pieces. If an enemy ship can stay in a blind area away from its opponent's fixed gunports, the ship cannot defend itself. Designs for armoring warships concentrated on these three areas and were paralleled by the development of movable turrets.

Everything that could possibly be plated was plated. For example, the smokestacks of some ships were armored since they had to remain intact to allow proper draft of the boiler fire. If riddled by gunfire, the smokestack would not draw properly, and the boiler fire would not burn hot enough to heat the boiler sufficiently. With reduced steam pressure, the ship's speed and maneuverability would be compromised.

The rudders, which regulate the ship's direction, were controlled from the pilot-

house through the use of chains attached to the rudders. If the chains were exposed, they could be struck and the ship would have no directional movement. If the ship were struck at or below the waterline, water would rush into the ship's interior and sink it. If the hole were not too large and there were time to put corrective measures in place, the ship could often be saved.

Naval Propulsion Systems

Most oceangoing vessels of the era had both a screw, or propeller, and sails to propel them. The screw was used to maneuver in tight places and to propel the ship when there was insufficient wind to use sails. The sails were used in the open ocean to conserve fuel and in the event the steam engine

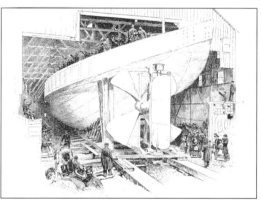

LEFT: The USS Onondaga *patrolling on the James River in Virginia. The* Onondaga *was one of the later double-turreted river monitors, commissioned in March 1864. She mounted two 15-inch (38.1cm) smoothbores and two 150-pounder (68.1kg) rifles. She saw action throughout the war and was sold to France in 1867. Painting by William R. McGrath. ABOVE: Stern view of the single-turret monitor USS* Dictator *showing the giant single screw and rudder used to propel and steer the boat. She had a complement of 174 officers and men, crammed into a hull only 312 feet (95.1m) long, 50 feet (15.2m) wide, and 20 feet (6.1m) deep. Built in November 1864, she served in the Atlantic Blockading Squadron.*

ceased to function. The steam engine was driven by a coal-fired boiler. In the Confederate Navy, the fuel of choice was hard, or anthracite, coal, since it gave off very little smoke, making ships difficult to see at a distance on the ocean. Soft, or bituminous, coal was used in Union vessels. Soft coal gave off a dark brown smoke that was easily seen, even at a distance.

Ships used in inland waterway naval operations were usually of the screw-driven or paddle wheel variety. Many naval ships were converted from commercial paddle wheel river steamers. The large paddle wheels were mounted at the stern on one or both sides or amidships, depending on the design of the vessel. The paddle wheel was one of the first motive designs for steam-powered ships. It was very useful in shallow waters where the depth of the keel is critical, but it could also be used on oceangoing craft. When propeller design was understood and implemented, screw-driven ships were used in the open ocean because the screw was more efficient, but had to be set down in the water to do its job properly.

The steam engine took some time to be put into service. Its firebox had to be filled with coal and ignited. The cold boiler, filled with water, had to be heated to a high temperature in order to generate sufficient steam to consistently run the engine at full throttle. One of the worst conditions a ship could find itself in during an engagement was the "steam down" position. In steam down, the boiler was kept at a low pressure, with sufficient fire to keep steam in the boiler, but not enough to move the ship at any significant speed. This was done primarily to conserve fuel on a ship that was not expected to move. If a Confederate blockade-runner passed a Union picket ship that was in steam-down status, there was simply no sense in the Union ship's even attempting pursuit. The time that it would take for the ship to "steam up" was more than enough to allow the blockade-runner, already under full steam, to get clean away.

Coal was always problematic as a fuel. It was very bulky and very heavy, and it had to be transported to the ships from mining sites in the Appalachian Mountains. Wood was used in early steamers on the rivers, but coal was found to be the superior fuel. Only coal, it seemed, provided a fire hot enough to ensure adequate steam pressure in newer engines. Only in emergencies would other, less desirable fuels such as wood be used. In the open ocean, coaling ships carried the coal to men-of-war, shuttling between the shore and the operating vessels. On the inland waters of the West, such as the Mississippi River, coal barges were towed or pushed up and down the river to the needy vessels. In some cases on the inland waters, a warship would lash a coal barge to its side in order to carry its fuel with it.

Life Aboard Ship

Life aboard a mid-nineteenth-century warship was difficult. There was little room for excess baggage or personal belongings. Men slept in hammocks suspended from interior rigging or on the deck of the ship. Generally, only the captain of the vessel and his officers had private cabins. Space in a warship was needed for survival supplies, munitions, food, and water. Contagious diseases (e.g., smallpox, cholera, and "fever") could and did sweep rapidly through the closely quartered ship's company. Sometimes diseases of malnutrition (e.g., scurvy or pellagra) could incapacitate an entire crew, rendering it ineffective for combat. There was no hospital room aboard ship; the sick lay on the deck until they recovered—or perished. In a couple of situations, there were Union hospital ships available, usually for army casualties, but these ships never had sufficient capacity to handle all the wounded.

The USS Planter, *a supply boat used to transport medical supplies, is shown here at Appomattox Landing, Virginia. The* Planter, *which originally belonged to a Southern plantation owner, was stolen by a slave pilot, John Small, and delivered to Union naval forces in May 1862.*

Medical science, then in its infancy, could do little for the terrible wounds that resulted from most naval combat. The size and type of munitions used created ghastly wounds in naval personnel, and the lack of knowledge concerning proper infection control virtually guaranteed infection, mutilation, amputation, or death for the injured sailor.

In combat, sailors faced the usual hazards of shot and shell. Shot weighed anywhere from six to four hundred pounds (2.7kg–181.6kg) and could crush a man instantly. Shell exploded, sending fragments of hot steel all around. Steam boilers, if struck by a round, would explode, sending scalding steam throughout the enclosed ship. In some instances, the spiraling effect of rounds striking the exterior of the ship, along with the concussion, would send shards of wood flying among the sailors at their gun stations.

On many ships, the interior was painted white to aid vision when the ship was closed up for combat. In addition to the natural darkness, vision would be seriously impaired by clouds of gunsmoke once a battle began. Before a battle, sand would be liberally strewn on the ship's deck because guns were wiped down with water-soaked sponges between shots, and this water on the deck, along with blood from the wounded and killed, would make a shifting deck so slippery that the men could not stand up without the traction provided by the sand. If there were many wounded, the ship's surgeon would not be able to attend to them all. Many would lie moaning and screaming on the deck until the battle was over and they could be attended to by their comrades.

LEFT: Crew of a Sassacus-class, double-ended, sidewheel gunboat posed on her afterdeck. These wooden-hulled boats could steer in either direction thanks to a rudder built on each end of the ship. These lightly gunned, unarmored support ships worked well in shallow, inland waters but were unstable on the open sea. ABOVE: Many a sailor in early nineteenth-century America began his career at sea as a child. This young "powder monkey" had a dangerous job: during combat, he carried ammunition components from the stores to the gunners. He is posed against a rifle that has had its breech reinforced with a band to allow it to fire larger, more powerful powder charges, thus increasing its range and accuracy.

Naval tactics dictated that the vessels get as close to each other as possible and attempt, by smoothbore naval artillery or ramming, to incapacitate the other vessel. For this reason, most early naval battles were fought at very close range. Naval artillery duels sometimes took place with the vessels in physical contact with one another since most naval artillery was of the "battering" kind. A shot fired from too far might not

penetrate a ship's outer hull, or armor, and do the necessary damage. So the closer, the better. Of course, the closer you were, the better the chance the enemy's round had of penetrating your ship.

Once naval rifles came into use on ships, the range and tactics of battle changed. In the battle between the CSS *Alabama* and the USS *Kearsarge*, the two ships, after initially firing at a distance of one mile (1.6km), fought the battle at a range of five hundred yards (457m).

If necessary, sailors and sometimes selected infantry were prepared to leave their own vessel and board the enemy vessel to engage in hand-to-hand combat. While this was only an occasional occurrence, thought was given to the possibility in planning a ship's defenses. For example, in the Union's Mississippi River city-class ironclads, hoses were attached to the steam boiler so that scalding steam could be sprayed on any persons attempting to board the vessel.

A favorite tactic was ramming, and some ships were specially designed to be used as rams. Their prows were armored and their interior structure braced so that they might accept the collision and, it was hoped, escape significant harm. Normally, a collision at sea would put both vessels in danger of sinking, just as a highway collision is likely to wreck both vehicles. Rams had a tactical advantage in that they could try to run themselves into other ships at a strategic point such as the rudder, causing damage that would incapacitate the other ship or sink it.

In this William R. McGrath painting of one of the most famous sea battles of the war, the CSS Alabama, *captained by Commander Raphael Semmes, engages the USS* Kearsarge *off the coast of France. After a lengthy battle, the* Alabama *was sunk, ending her career as a notorious Confederate raider that targeted Union commercial shipping.*

chapter 1

1861
EARLY NAVAL OPERATIONS

FORT SUMTER

The Civil War is considered to have begun when South Carolina state troops fired on the Union garrison at Fort Sumter in the harbor at Charleston, South Carolina, on April 12, 1861. Prior to this moment, there had not been any serious confrontation between Union military forces and the forces of the seceding states. A lame-duck administration under President James Buchanan stood idly by while state after state seceded from the Union. Buchanan did not want to create any problems.

On January 5, 1861, a Federal force aboard the transport USS *Star of the West* steamed south from New York to relieve the U.S. troops stationed at Fort Sumter under Major Robert Anderson. Upon reaching the Charleston harbor, the *Star of the West* was fired on by South Carolina state militia guns and was forced to turn around and return north without accomplishing her mission. The relief of Fort Sumter was put on hold until the inauguration of Abraham Lincoln on March 4, 1861. Lincoln, newly elected, was also reluctant to force any issue with the southern states, at least until he had a chance to put his cabinet fully in place. Finally, in April, Lincoln ordered a ship of provisions sent to the beleaguered garrison. On April 12, 1861, after negotiations for surrender and evacuation had failed, the South Carolina guns opened fire on the fort, giving Lincoln the excuse he needed to place the United States on a war footing. On April 13, Anderson surrendered Fort Sumter to the Confederates.

"Our Southern Brethren have done grievously wrong, they have rebelled and have attacked their father's house and their loyal brothers. They must be punished and brought back, but this necessity breaks my heart."

—*Major Robert Anderson, commanding U.S. troops at the surrender of Fort Sumter, April 14, 1861*

PAGE 29: In this rare drawing, the CSS Sumter is seen leaving New Orleans in June 1861 for her successful cruise as a Confederate raider. In one of the earliest efforts to defeat the blockade against the South, the Sumter captured eighteen ships in a six-month period. ABOVE: James Buchanan, fifteenth president of the United States, was a lame duck from November 6, 1860, when Abraham Lincoln defeated Stephen A. Douglas, until March 4, 1861, when Lincoln took the oath of office. Buchanan did little to interfere with the secession of Southern states. During Buchanan's administration, on January 5, 1861, South Carolina militia gunners fired on an attempted Federal reinforcement of Fort Sumter.

The secessionist attack on Fort Sumter was not unexpected. Since Lincoln's election, the pre-election threats of secession by the southern states had begun to be implemented (Florida seceded on January 10, South Carolina on January 11). The U.S. military commanders did what they could in terms of planning for the expected conflict without creating political problems; Lincoln hoped he could keep the country together through

diplomacy. As it became clear that armed conflict was inevitable, Union naval commanders began considering those assets in the South that would fall into Confederate hands. Foremost among these assets was the naval facility at Norfolk, Virginia. It contained hundreds of cannon, including more than three hundred Dahlgren guns. In addition to naval stores and a first-class dock facility, it was also the berth for several Union men-of-war, including the USS *Merrimack,* a twenty-two-gun steam frigate.

On April 17, the Virginia legislature voted to secede and the U.S. Navy went into action, its first mission being the destruction of the Norfolk facility. Whether the ineptness of the commanding officer, Commodore Hiram Paulding, the intentional dereliction of loyal southern officers, or both, was responsible, the April 20 attempt to destroy the naval yard failed almost totally. All ships at anchor were burned, including the *Merrimack,* and some stores were destroyed, but, for the most part, the Confederates occupied a nearly intact naval yard. Many of the yard's cannon would be used to arm the forts hastily being constructed by the Confederates along rivers and bays and on the Atlantic Ocean.

SECESSION AND BLOCKADE

As state after state seceded from the Union, it became clear to both sides that war was imminent. Lincoln assigned the task of generating a master strategic plan to an aging but still able General Winfield Scott, hero of the Mexican War. Scott rightly believed that for the North to win, the under-industrialized South had to be kept from supplying and industrializing itself from any outside source. Since raw materials and machinery were scarce in the South and could not be obtained readily from the northern United

States, his plan was to choke off the South from the western areas of the United States and from the outside world just as a constricting snake chokes its victim. From this principle came Scott's plan, sometimes derisively referred to as the "Anaconda Plan," which called for a total blockade of all southern ports, complete control over all the river infrastructure in the South, and total naval superiority. Scott felt that without outside supply the South would be forced to capitulate when its supplies ran out (he estimated three years), and combat with the southern states might not even be necessary. Lincoln adopted the blockade aspect of the plan and immediately ordered his tiny national navy to blockade all thirty-five hundred miles (5,600km) of southern coastline and take control of the Mississippi River and all of its many tributaries.

The Union, unprepared for war though it was, began piecemeal implementation of the blockade plan. One by one, southern ports were blockaded, often with only one ship. In the Mississippi River area, Union ships slowly began cruising the waters in an effort to curtail Confederate commerce and test the Confederate defenses at various locations. The rivers in the West were critically important. There was very poor road infrastructure in the South, and most commerce moved on the few railroads and along the many rivers of the area. Control of the river infrastructure was critical if the Union was to have any chance of defeating the Confederate forces in the West using Scott's plan.

The most critical area on the Confederate Atlantic coast was the area of Hampton Roads. Sitting between the Accomack peninsula and Virginia Beach, Hampton Roads controlled all egress from the Chesapeake Bay and Virginia ports to the Atlantic Ocean. Any Confederate ships north of Wilmington and Hatteras would have to put in to these ports; by the same token, any

In the early morning hours of September 9, 1863, landing parties from the blockading Federal fleet attempted a small-boat assault against Confederate forces manning Fort Sumter. The Union raiders met with heavy fire, and the assault failed, with 135 Union casualties.

ships leaving these ports would have to run the gauntlet of Union warships that took up positions in Hampton Roads.

With the announcement of the blockade, the Confederate Secretary of the Navy, Stephen R. Mallory, realized that his naval operations would have a twofold mission: to fight the U.S. Navy and to supply the

Confederacy with its material needs. With too much coastline to defend and not enough ships of the line, Mallory decided on a coastal defense strategy that relied on building forts at critical locations while keeping the Confederate navy mobile. In addition to his man-of-war construction scheme, he sought and obtained several ships whose

designs enabled them to achieve high speeds in the open ocean. These blockade-runners were to be the lifeline of the Confederacy: they would carry southern goods, chiefly cotton, to European or Caribbean markets (Nassau, Havana, Bermuda), and trade these goods for war matériel. At first the Confederate Navy was heavily involved in

On the night of April 20, 1861, Federal naval personnel at the Norfolk, Virginia, Navy Yard (usually called Gosport) evacuated the facility. Although they attempted to destroy all boats, materials, and docks that could be of use to the Confederates, they failed to destroy the facility completely, and Gosport was put to significant use by the Confederate Navy.

blockade-running. As soon as the trade established itself as profitable, most of the blockade-running business was turned over to private enterprise, although the government continued to receive a percentage of the value of each cargo.

Blockade-runners were operated by businessmen who received large profits from the southern population. The ships were carefully designed and well built, and many of them were paddle-wheelers. Some had telescoping smokestacks, which allowed the ship to change its profile and to lessen its wind drag when under sail. Another technique in use was the removable screw, which was raised out of the water by its shaft once the ship was on the open ocean, further reducing water drag when under sail. The less fuel that had to be carried, the more room for cargo, leading to greater profit.

The reduction and capture of the southern ports, one by one, coupled with the reduction in available landing sites for the blockade-runners, made blockade-running all but impossible by late 1864. It became clear that blockade-running was no longer profitable when the Confederate government ceased to demand its percentage of the value of the cargo, it no longer being worthwhile. During its heyday, however, blockade-running made some people very wealthy; a single trip could pay for the ship, and one runner is known to have made forty-two trips.

PRIVATEERS

To encourage private parties to join the Confederacy's struggle, President Jefferson Davis began issuing Letters of Marque and Reprisal in April 1861. Letters of Marque and Reprisal were individual privateering permits allowing a civilian, under the auspices of the government of a belligerent nation, to attack the commercial and military vessels of the enemy and of neutral nations (if they were carrying contraband bound for the enemy). The civilian ships, called privateers, were allowed to keep the captured ship and its cargo if they could return it to one of their country's ports and have it adjudicated as theirs by a prize court. The ship and its cargo then became a "prize." Prizes were usually distributed on a percentage basis among the ship's owners, officers, and crew. Privateers were generally armed with cannon and small arms.

There was a great deal of concern about privateers in the North, where they were

On March 17, 1862, the cruiser CSS Nashville *slipped out of Beaufort, North Carolina, to raid Union shipping. In September 1861 she had become the first Confederate warship to arrive in European waters. Late in 1862, she was sold as a blockade-runner and renamed the* Thomas L. Wragg. *Early the following year, she was recommissioned as a privateer, the* Rattlesnake; *she was destroyed by the monitor USS* Montauk *on the Ogeechee River in Georgia in February 1863.*

Although derided by many, including the press, General Winfield Scott's plan to economically strangle the South into submission by means of a blockade ultimately succeeded. This pro-Union political cartoon from an Ohio newspaper pokes fun at Scott's plan.

decried as pirates and criminals. Most of the major European nations had abolished privateering against each other in the 1856 Treaty of Paris. After the U.S. Navy had stopped and seized several British vessels coming from southern ports, the British government called on the U.S. government to stop the practice. The U.S. government officially notified the British government that a blockade was in place against the seceding Confederate states and that a state of war existed. Once notified, the major European powers declared their neutrality and opened their ports to both belligerents' navies, including privateers. However, no privateer could discharge or sell its cargo in a neutral port.

Chasing down Confederate blockade-runners at night, especially in bad weather, was not an easy chore. However, as the war progressed and more blockaders prowled the Atlantic ports, Confederate successes dwindled.

The U.S. government tried unsuccessfully to get the British government to reopen the negotiations of the Treaty of Paris so that the United States could join the antiprivateering decision and thereby bar Confederate privateers from using foreign harbors. Some of the privateers were operated by British and other foreign crews, who were quick to recognize that the situation presented immense opportunities for profit.

THE TRENT AFFAIR

One of the war's most anxious moments occurred on the high seas in October 1861.

On October 12, the same day the *St. Louis* was launched into the Mississippi River, two Confederate diplomats, John Slidell and James M. Mason, were spirited out of the Charleston harbor on the blockade-runner *Theodora* bound for Havana, a transshipment point to England, where they were to be the emissaries of the Confederate government.

U.S. Secretary of State Seward, upon hearing of their escape from the United States and thinking they were aboard a Confederate vessel, the CSS *Nashville,* ordered that they be captured.

On November 8, the USS *San Jacinto,* under the command of Captain Charles Wilkes, found Mason, Slidell, and their families at Havana, waiting for transportation aboard a British mail packet, the *Trent.* Lying off the Havana harbor, Wilkes waited until the *Trent* had made her exit. On the high seas, the *San Jacinto* forced the *Trent* to heave to and be boarded. Despite the obvious illegality of the act, Union sailors boarded the *Trent,* seized Slidell and Mason, and took them to the *San Jacinto.*

On November 24, Wilkes arrived at Boston with Mason and Slidell, who were immediately imprisoned at Fort Warren in Boston Harbor. Newspapers and politicians were jubilant over the capture. By the end of the next week, England was ablaze with indignation over the flagrant violation of British sovereignty. The British government, through its minister in Washington, Lord Lyons, demanded the release of Mason and Slidell coupled with an appropriate apology. On December 19, Lord Lyons communicated the demand to Secretary of State Seward along with notification that if an answer was

In this contemporary drawing, Captain Charles Wilkes of the USS San Jacinto *boards the British mail packet* Trent *and takes Confederate commissioners John Slidell and James M. Mason into his custody. This incident, commonly referred to as the Trent Affair, severely strained relations between the United States and Britain. At the last hour, Lincoln released Mason and Slidell to continue their journey to England.*

The USS San Jacinto *fires a round across the bow of the British mail packet* Trent, *ordering the foreign vessel to heave to and prepare to be boarded.*

Captain Charles Wilkes, *captain of the USS* San Jacinto *during the Trent Affair.*

not forthcoming in seven days, the British ambassador and his entourage would leave the United States.

Jubilation turned to concern as the U.S. government realized that Britain, already considered friendly to the Confederate States, might feel compelled to take military and diplomatic action against the United States. On December 20, two British warships loaded with troops set sail for Canada to add emphasis to Lyons' demands.

The Confederate government had vehemently protested against the seizure of Slidell and Mason, and used the incident to create a closer bond between the Confederate States and Britain. Lyons met again with Seward on December 21 and 23, underscoring the possibility of Britain entering into a war against the United States. Finally, on December 26, the final day allowed by the British government, the Lincoln administration caved in, admitting that the seizure was illegal, and released Mason and Slidell to continue their trip to England. The Confederate government saw the opportunity to bring the British into the war slip from their grasp.

THE BEGINNING OF COMBINED SEA/LAND OPERATIONS

On the coastal waters of the South, Union naval commanders were beginning the slow, arduous job of working in uncharted waters. One of their first tasks along the Carolina coast was to explore the myriad bays, inlets, and rivers. These relatively shallow waterways provided excellent ports for the shallow-draft blockade-runners. In order to deny their use to the enemy, the Union Navy had to navigate deep-draft warships in these treacherous waters.

In August 1861, in accordance with the blockade order, the Union Navy continued to

Rear Admiral Samuel F. DuPont, an experienced naval officer, was assigned the unenviable task of blockading the South's Atlantic ports at the beginning of the war.

Major General Benjamin F. Butler, a New Hampshire politician and militia commander, assisted in the assault on Fort Hatteras in 1861. After an ill-fated expedition against Fort Fisher, North Carolina, in December 1864, in which he left six hundred Union troops stranded on a beach, he was relieved of command by Lieutenant General U.S. Grant.

carry out its plan to reduce selected critical southern coastal fortifications and harbors. Commodore Silas H. Stringham was placed in command of a squadron composed of seven armed ships and three transports containing nine hundred infantry troops under the command of Major General Benjamin F. Butler. The purpose of this squadron was to destroy and capture forts Hatteras and Clark, which controlled Hatteras Inlet, North Carolina, and the major sounds and rivers within the protection of the Hatteras barrier islands. This area was chosen because it offered the Confederacy a natural blockade-runner port that could supply other southern areas. The two main rivers, the Neuse and the Pamlico, allowed a protected site for blockade-runners to put up and restock.

In this drawing by Alfred Waud, Union troops are shown landing on North Carolina's Outer Banks during the assault on forts Clark and Hatteras in August 1861. This was the first combined sea and land operation in U.S. military history.

The U.S. Marine Corps saw limited action in the great land battles of the Civil War, but marines served an invaluable role as the offensive arm of the Federal blockade of the Southern coast. In this painting by Don Troiani, marines advance up a beach on the North Carolina coast in one of the countless amphibious raids that helped to enforce the blockade.

A posed photograph of U.S. sailors servicing a large smoothbore cannon aboard a warship. Each man is at his battle station. Note the gunner, who uses his thumb to cover the primer port on the cannon to prevent an accidental discharge. The sailors wearing the corrugated waist protectors used their body weight to belay the ropes when moving the gun back into position.

On August 27, 1861, Stringham's squadron, consisting of the warships *Minnesota, Wabash, Monticello, Susquehanna, Pawnee,* and *Cumberland,* and a revenue steamer, the *Harriet Lane,* bearing a total of 158 guns, arrived in the vicinity of Cape Hatteras. Early on the morning of August 28, they opened fire on the two forts. The transports *Adelaide, George Peabody,* and *Fanny* lay offshore out of range of the forts' twenty-five guns. The technique used to reduce the forts was to form the warships in a line and sail in an ellipse within cannon range of Fort Clark, the outermost fort. In this way, the ships were able to fire continuous, though somewhat inaccurate, broadsides into the fort, while at the same time offering more difficult targets to the land-based gunners within the forts. Concurrent with the naval attack, a contingent of infantry was landed north of the forts, where it would be in a position to storm the facilities once they had been sufficiently reduced by the naval gunfire.

*TOP: The CSS **Florida**, a blockade-runner and cruiser, is shown in this contemporary French engraving in the port of Brest, France. ABOVE: The CSS **Robert E. Lee** was famous for successfully running the blockade twenty-two times before she was captured by U.S. ships off Bermuda in 1863. She was taken into the U.S. Navy and renamed USS **Fort Donelson**. She went on to work the blockading squadron, chasing down her former comrades. Capable of eleven knots (5.7 m/sec), she boasted telescoping smokestacks and twin paddle wheels.*

Having reduced the forts, the Union Army found that occupying them was a little harder to accomplish than they had thought. Within a month, on September 29, three thousand Confederate troops aboard several vessels steamed to Hatteras Island in an effort to cut off and capture six hundred troops of the 20th Indiana who had been sent to occupy Chicamacomico on the northern end of Hatteras Island. The Union troops were warned in the nick of time and managed, through hard marching in deep sand, and with the help of a naval artillery barrage from the USS *Monticello*, to avoid capture and return to the fort.

Following the capture of Fort Hatteras, two naval squadrons were formed in place of the Union's Atlantic Squadron. Admiral Goldsborough was placed in command of the North Atlantic Squadron, responsible for the coast of Virginia and North Carolina, and Admiral Samuel DuPont was placed in command of the South Atlantic Squadron, responsible for the coast from South Carolina to the southern cape of Florida.

BATTLE OF THE MISSISSIPPI PASSES

In late 1861, U.S. Navy operations in the Gulf of Mexico were concentrated on the former U.S. naval base at Pensacola, Florida, the multichanneled mouth of the Mississippi River, and the Confederate ports in Texas. The Mississippi River delta was formed from the river's sediment, which, through the centuries, had reduced the Mississippi's mouth from a single waterway into a series of smaller waterways spread out in the shape of a fan. This geographical situation made it virtually impossible for the USS *Brooklyn* to control the area without additional vessels. In October 1861, four additional ships, the

By midmorning, the colors had been struck by the Confederate troops manning Fort Clark. Union troops moved forward and occupied the fort, which they found abandoned. With Fort Clark in their possession, the attention of the Union armada was turned next to Fort Hatteras. A sandbar across the mouth of Hatteras Inlet prevented the deep-draft Union naval ships from entering the inlet. On the morning of August 29, these ships moved south and set up anchored positions at the southern end of the inlet. From that position, they proceeded to conduct a continuous naval bombardment of Fort Hatteras. Around 11 A.M., the Confederates in the fort sent up a white flag, and an unconditional surrender of the fort and its personnel was effected. The Confederate prisoners were placed aboard the transports and taken to prison on Governor's Island, New York. The forts were then occupied by troops of the 20th Indiana Regiment.

Commissioned just before the war began, the screw sloop USS Richmond *stayed in combat throughout the war, fighting in some of the toughest contests in the West. At the beginning of the war, during the Battle of Sabine Passes, she was struck by the Confederate ram CSS* Manassas.

Richmond, the Vincennes, the Preble, and the small screw steamer Water Witch, arrived to block the passes of the Mississippi. They totaled forty-seven guns, and were considered capable of handling anything the Confederates might have in the area, and of preventing blockade-runners and commerce raiders from gaining the open sea.

On October 13, 1861, in the dark of the morning, a small Confederate flotilla from New Orleans, consisting of the Ivy, the Tuscarora, the Calhoun, the Jackson, the ram Manassas, and a towboat, the Watson, under the command of Commodore J.S. Hollins, steamed their way to the position of the Union Navy. The USS Richmond was taking on coal from a coaler and since the ship's crew was busy loading coal, no lookout had been posted. In the nearly impenetrable darkness, the ram Manassas took a full head of steam and headed for the position of the Union ships, hoping to ram one or more of them. Suddenly, the Richmond and the coaler loomed out of the darkness directly in front of the Manassas. Lieutenant A.F. Warley, commanding the Manassas, rammed his ship directly into the coaling schooner and the Richmond, causing damage to the Richmond but crippling his own ship in the process.

Recovering quickly from the surprise, the Union ships came to general quarters and opened a fusillade of cannon fire on the Confederate ships. Warley extracted his now-damaged ram from the side of the Richmond and beat a slow but regular retreat to a nearby shoreline. The Confederate ships, some armed with Whitworth rifles, fired into the milling Union ships. In the dark, few of the rounds from either side found their mark. Finally, the Tuscarora and the Watson delivered five fire barges into the stream floating toward the Union fleet. This succeeded in breaking contact between the two forces.

The oddly shaped but effective Confederate ram CSS Manassas. The first all-metal ship built by the Confederacy, she was cigar-shaped and sat very low in the water. She was run aground by the USS Mississippi but salvaged by her crew, and she fought at the Battle of New Orleans.

A fire barge was a device designed for use against wooden ships such as those anchored off the Mississippi passes that morning. A simple floating barge was filled with flammable materials, usually wood, hay, and pitch, and towed to the scene of the fighting. It was maneuvered upstream from the enemy, set on fire, and allowed to float down and into the enemy ships. The size of the fire was so great that any ship that came into contact with it was likely to catch fire. Fire aboard a wooden sailing ship was a great peril, since there were few, if any, methods of putting out a fire, particularly if the crew were at their battle stations defending against other warships.

Morning found the Manassas lying concealed along the shore and the Tuscarora and the Watson grounded on bars. Some miles south, the Richmond and the Vincennes had gone hard aground on a bar, and the other Union ships had formed into a defensive perimeter to take advantage of the Richmond's guns. The remaining Confederate boats floated to within gun range and engaged the Union ships in an exchange of cannon fire. However, neither side suffered significant damage, and the Confederates eventually withdrew.

During this exchange of fire, a comedy of errors on the Union side nearly ended in disaster. Captain Robert Handy, commander of the USS Vincennes, misunderstood a signal from Captain John Pope of the Richmond. Believing that he had been ordered to abandon and destroy his ship, Handy immediately ordered his men into boats and placed a slow fuse on the powder magazine. When Handy arrived aboard the Richmond and reported to Captain Pope, he had the national ensign from the Vincennes wrapped around his waist like a sash. After a brief inquiry, an apoplectic Captain Pope ordered Handy back to the Vincennes. It was discovered that the seaman ordered to light the fuse on the magazine had not done so, and there was no danger of explosion. The next day, the Richmond and the Vincennes were pulled from the bar and took up their positions on picket duty.

chapter 2

1862
NAVAL WAR IN THE WEST

IRONCLADS, RAMS, AND TRANSPORTS

Control of the Mississippi River was critical to the Union plan to starve the Confederacy into submission. As long as the Mississippi was not controlled completely by the U.S. Navy, Confederate forces could receive supplies, men, and matériel from the states west of the Mississippi. At the outset of the war, Union strategic planners felt that the gunboats on the Mississippi should be under the operational control of the U.S. Army, since the U.S. Navy was considered to be an exclusively blue-water (oceangoing) navy. Although the navy provided officers to staff the gunboats, it was not until October 1862 that operational control of the ironclads was transferred to the navy.

By the summer of 1861, plans were well under way for the production of twelve to twenty new ironclad river vessels for the U.S. Army. Samuel Pook modified an original design by James Lenthall, and the boats were contracted to be built by James Eads at a new Union shipyard at Mound City, Illinois, near Cairo. Pook's plan called for a massive flat-bottomed paddle wheeler, fifty feet (15.2m) wide by 175 feet (53.3m) long and drawing only six feet (1.8m) of water. On the hull of the boat, a casemate constructed of thick oak and iron plate was to run completely around the vessel. The sides of the vessel sloped at thirty-five degrees, while the front and rear sloped at forty-five degrees. The combination of angle and iron was enough to defeat most cannon.

These new ironclads mounted massive naval artillery. The USS *Cairo*, for example,

"The loss of the rebels must be very heavy; their vessels were literally torn to pieces, and some had holes in their sides through which a man could walk. Those that blew up—it makes me shudder to think of them."

—Lieutenant S.L. Phelps, commander of the ironclad gunboat USS *Benton*, regarding the naval action at *Plum Point, May 10, 1862*

PAGE 45: *The cotton-clad Confederate Mississippi River Defense Fleet rams crash into the Union ironclad fleet at Plum Point in May 1862. In the ensuing close-quarter combat, several ironclads were rammed and sunk. The Confederates suffered losses as well, presaging the doom of the river defense fleet less than a month later.* **ABOVE:** *The only known wartime photograph of the USS* Cairo, *a city-class ironclad. The* Cairo *was sunk by Confederate mines on December 12, 1862, in the Yazoo River in Mississippi. She was recovered by the National Park Service in 1964 and put on display at Vicksburg National Military Park.*

mounted three 42-pounder (19kg) army rifles, three 64-pounder (29kg) navy smoothbores, six 32-pounder (14.5kg) navy smoothbores, and one 32-pounder (14.5kg) Parrott gun. The guns were arranged three in the bow ports, four on each side, and two in the stern ports. The ship was operated by seventeen officers and 158 enlisted men. After dealing with strikes, supply problems, and other delays, Eads delivered the *Cairo* on

January 15, 1862, ninety days past schedule. In total, only seven of the Eads city-class ironclads were built.

Another novel form of naval vessel in the Mississippi River area was the tinclad. Tinclads were lightly armored river vessels, side and rear paddle wheelers with a shallow draft, many of which had previously been commercial transports. They were armored with quarter-inch (0.6cm) steel around critical

areas, and they used cotton bales, timber, and other materials to help absorb the force of any fire they received. There were a total of sixty-three tinclads on the Mississippi River, each bearing her serial number on the side of the wheelhouse. They were armed with an assortment of cannon. The USS *Marmora* was originally armed with two 24-pounder (10.8kg) smoothbores and two 12-pounder (5.4kg) rifles. The USS *Signal,* dur-

Admiral David Glasgow Farragut, began his naval career as a boy and worked his way to the top of his profession.

reinforced so that they would survive the shock of hitting another vessel at speed. The bows were reinforced and filled with timber. The rams were somewhat unusual in that most of them carried no naval artillery. Ellet commanded the ram fleet, and it remained a U.S. Army unit throughout the war, operating as an independent command. Although Ellet's rams operated under naval orders, there was some resentment on the part of naval officers over the fact that army officers had been placed in command of boats in a naval flotilla.

Yet another of the specialized river vessels was the mortar scow. The mortar scow was a raft with sides carrying a mortar. A mortar is a weapon with a high angle of fire, used for indirect fire on protected targets. By firing its round high into the air, it can strike areas which are protected from direct cannon fire, such as the interior of a fort. These mortar scows were not self-powered, and they had to be pulled into position by other craft.

In addition to the mortar scows, there was a small fleet of powered schooners that carried mortars. These, originally commanded by Admiral David Dixon Porter, U.S.N., at the Battle of New Orleans, were kept with the fleet of Naval Officer David Glasgow Farragut, and were used repeatedly on the lower end of the Mississippi River and in the Gulf of Mexico.

After General Ulysses S. Grant's victory at forts Henry and Donelson, the idea of moving troops by naval craft and using naval gunfire in support of the infantry became an integral part of his strategy. In the summer and fall of 1862, in preparation for further operations against Southern strongholds, the government purchased or leased numerous commercial paddle wheel river steamboats. These boats were used as troop transports and bore neither armor nor cannon.

Even as early as 1862, the Union advantage in men and matériel was beginning to show in the West. Large Union forces pushed

ing the same period, was armed with two 30-pounder (13.6kg) rifles, four 24-pounder (10.8kg) howitzers, and one 12-pounder (5.4kg) rifle. The size of the tinclads' crews varied widely depending on the size of the vessel and the number of personnel available.

In 1862 there were two ways to sink a boat with another boat. You could shoot it until it sank, or you could ram it. There was, of course, a serious downside to the latter option: unless the ramming boat was specially prepared, it usually suffered as much damage as the boat rammed. A U.S. Army officer, Charles Ellet, came up with the idea of reinforcing certain boats and using them to intentionally ram enemy ships. Logically enough, these special boats were called rams. Ellet convinced the army's Quartermaster Department to purchase seven river steamers and have them converted to his specifications. The interior frames of the rams were

*The USS **Cincinnati**, another of the city-class ironclads built by James Eads, was twice sunk and raised during the war, and saw action in the western theater. The colored bands on the smokestacks identified the city-class ironclads.*

Lieutenant General Ulysses S. Grant, commander of land forces in the western theater, later went on to lead all the Union armies and to accept Lee's surrender at Appomattox.

Captain David Dixon Porter became commander of Union naval operations in the Mississippi River after Henry Walke fell ill.

Confederate General Lloyd Tilghman, commander of the defenders at Fort Henry, was killed in action at Champion's Hill, Mississippi in May 1863.

the Confederates out of Kentucky by March. Although General Henry Halleck was in overall command of the western district, Grant was the major tactical commander. Grant knew that the lack of interior lines of communication in the rural South meant that he had to depend significantly on naval transport. This dependency led, in part, to a friendship between Grant and Porter. This friendship in turn contributed greatly to the development of the doctrine of combined army and naval operation.

In late January 1862, President Lincoln took a bold step to get the inactive Union forces into combat. He issued General War Order Number 1, declaring that all Union forces should move against the enemy on February 22. Modifying Scott's "wait and starve" theory, Lincoln hoped that a concerted drive against the Confederates would strain

their limited resources and bring about their surrender. He was to be very disappointed, however, as most of his commanders showed a lack of resolve and an inability to take the offensive, while the enemy displayed tremendous spirit and tenacity.

FORTS HENRY AND DONELSON: CONTINUED DEVELOPMENT OF COMBINED OPERATIONS

Grant told Halleck that his plan was to proceed against Fort Henry on the Tennessee River. With Halleck's approval and the support of the navy, Grant embarked on his campaign. His plan was to assault Fort Henry from the land side with ten thousand troops

while the navy's new ironclad gunboats shelled the fort from the river. On February 5, 1862, a cold and rainy day, Grant's operation began. His troops were delivered in two groups because of the shortage of transports. The naval forces under Commodore William D. Porter consisted of three of the new Eads ironclads (the *Carondelet,* the *Cincinnati,* and the *St. Louis*), a converted river steamer, the *Essex,* and three wooden ships (the *Conestoga,* the *Tyler,* and the *Lexington*). Fort Henry commanded a straight two-mile (3.2km) stretch of the Tennessee River. This forced the Union ships to fight the fort bow on, which meant that only their bow guns could be brought into action. Fort Henry had seventeen guns, twelve of which were trained on the river. The Union fleet could only bring about seventeen of their total seventy-six guns into action.

*The USS **Lexington** was one of the timberclad gunboats that gave naval gunfire support to Union army forces at Shiloh.*

The Union gunboats moved to within a third of a mile (0.5km) of the fort and began their cannonade. For an hour and a half the duel between the fort and the ironclads raged. Finally, the Confederate commander, General Lloyd Tilghman, his guns dismounted and his crews wounded by the continuous bombardment from the fleet, sent up the white flag. The shooting ceased, and Tilghman surrendered his garrison to the U.S. Navy. Captain Henry Walke went ashore and took custody of Fort Henry until Grant, whose troops had been seriously delayed by the flooded lowlands and by Confederate infantry, arrived some time later and took control.

During the battle for Fort Henry, the first fight in the West between ironclad gunboats and land-based weapons, the utility of the ironclad vessels was proven once again. The gunboats were struck repeatedly by accurate Confederate fire, but their armor held up against the onslaught. Only one, the *Essex*, suffered any serious damage, when she was hit by a shot that pierced the boiler and sent scalding steam through the ship, killing or wounding twenty-nine men.

Immediately upon taking control of Fort Henry, Grant reorganized his forces and declared his intention to take Fort Donelson, a nearby Confederate bastion located on the Cumberland River. Flag Officer A.H. Foote, U.S.N., reformed his fleet and replaced the damaged *Essex* with another Eads ironclad, the *Pittsburg*. On the afternoon of February 14, his fleet began the bombardment of Fort Donelson. The fort was defended by sixty-five guns and twenty-one thousand men. It was situated on top of a hundred-foot (30.4m) bluff and was protected by well-designed fortifications.

Foote's fleet moved to within four hundred yards (365.7m) of the fort and suffered severe damage. The *St. Louis* and the *Louisville* had their steering shot away and went adrift. The *Pittsburg* and the *Carondelet* were not able to withstand the fire from the fort's batteries and were severely damaged. After an hour and a half, the fleet withdrew from the fight. Each of Foote's vessels had been struck about fifty times with heavy shot, and the fleet had suffered fifty-four men killed or wounded.

On February 16, Grant's troops occupied Fort Donelson and took twelve thousand prisoners, pushing the Confederate line of defense further south. On February 17, a delighted President Lincoln appointed Grant commander of the new military territory of Western Tennessee. For the Confederacy, the loss of forts Henry and Donelson was a disaster. Their loss forced the evacuation, on February 20, of the fortifications at Columbus, Kentucky, which controlled part of the upper Mississippi River.

It was obvious by this point that the Union strategy was to work toward the complete closure of the Mississippi River. The collapse of the Confederate line in Kentucky opened the way for Union incursions deep into Tennessee and, collaterally, along the Mississippi River. The next step for the Union forces was to begin the point-by-point reduction of Confederate strongholds at both ends of the Mississippi.

SHILOH, OR PITTSBURG LANDING

By early April, Grant's army had moved into lower Tennessee and encamped near Pittsburg Landing, close to a small church called Shiloh Meeting House. Confederate forces under General Albert Sidney Johnston, recently forced out of Kentucky, regrouped at Corinth, Mississippi, south of Grant's position. On April 2, Johnston ordered his forty thousand soldiers to march against Grant's position at Pittsburg Landing.

Grant had used river transports to move his troops to Pittsburg Landing, and the ironclads used the landing as a staging point for further reconnaissance down the Tennessee River and its tributaries. One such reconnaissance went as far as Chickasaw, Alabama, and Eastport, Tennessee.

On April 6, Johnston's forty thousand troops fell upon Grant's unsuspecting infantry force of forty-two thousand, and the battle was on. Initially, the Confederates made significant gains, but they were eventually prevented from destroying Grant's army or occupying Pittsburg Landing. One key ingredient in the Union victory was Grant's ability to use navy transports to land infantry reinforcements at the landing, placing fresh troops near the fighting.

A contemporary popular depiction of Grant's army standing against the onslaught of Confederate infantry at Shiloh.

At the critical juncture of the battle, when Confederate forces massed for a final attack on the beleaguered Union troops, the USS *Tyler* and the USS *Lexington* took up positions near the bank of the Tennessee River and the left wing of the Union defenders. As the attack began, the ships opened fire with their guns and howitzers, pouring nearly four hundred rounds into the Confederate line between 6:00 P.M. and 5:00 A.M. the following morning. Some historians maintain that without the naval gunfire supporting them, the Union infantry would have been overrun. Whether or not this is the case, the utility of combined naval and infantry operations was clearly demonstrated.

BATTLE OF NEW ORLEANS

Prior to the outbreak of hostilities, New Orleans, the largest city in the South, was a major shipbuilding depot for the U.S. Navy. Its ideal location at the mouth of the Mississippi River made it a natural harbor for the transshipment of materials from ocean-going vessels to river vessels, and for the construction and repair of ships. The Confederates lost no time in putting these facilities to good use when they seized the naval yards and forts in January 1861. After the skirmish at the passes of the Mississippi River in October 1861, Lincoln knew that he had to take New Orleans to control the mouth of the Mississippi River above the passes. In November a plan was drawn up, set for execution in April 1862.

At New Orleans, the Union naval attack was expected. Two large forts, Fort Jackson and Fort St. Phillip, guarded a bend in the Mississippi River fifteen miles (24km) below New Orleans. Confederate defenders based their defense on these two old but substantial structures, combined with a makeshift blockade constructed of old ship hulls strung

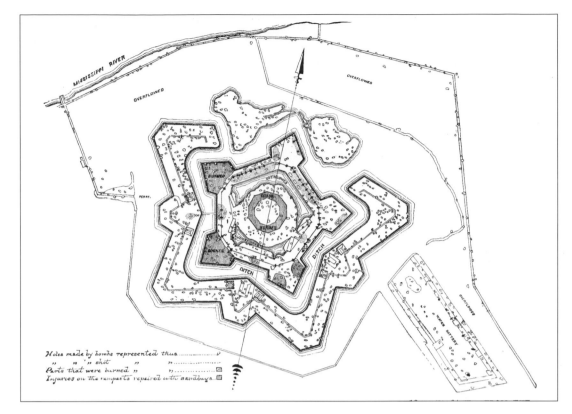

In an early form of bomb damage assessment, this engineer's drawing of Fort Jackson, which guarded the Mississippi River south of New Orleans, shows the locations of shell holes, marks, and other damage caused by the Union naval bombardment.

together on a chain across the river. If the Union fleet approached and passed the forts, the chained ships were to stop it and make it a sitting target for the forts' guns.

The original plan for the attack on New Orleans was conceived by Commodore Porter. This officer, however, was too junior in rank to lead the attack, and he was given responsibility only for the mortar schooner fleet. President Lincoln chose David Glasgow Farragut to lead the assault on the lower Mississippi River. Farragut was one of the navy's most experienced senior officers; he had begun his career in the War of 1812 as a ten-year-old midshipman aboard a naval man-of-war.

In secret, Farragut and Porter began assembling the necessary men and ships for

the expedition. Naval Secretary Welles, to cover Farragut's assignment, divided the Gulf Blockading Squadron into two parts, East and West, assigning Farragut responsibility for everything from the Rio Grande River at the Texas-Mexico border to Saint Andrew's Bay in Florida.

The New Orleans task force set out, and by February 1862 most of the fleet was assembled in the Gulf of Mexico. On March 1, Farragut sent a party into Biloxi, Mississippi, to raid the local post office and other shops for information. Through this, he received word of the Union victories at Fort Donelson and Fort Henry, and of the advance against Island Number 10 (see page 56). The way was paved for an assault on the Mississippi River and New Orleans.

NAVAL WAR IN THE WEST

OPPOSITE: *Admiral Farragut's flagship, the USS* Hartford, *runs the guns in front of Fort Jackson, Louisiana. Painting by Tom W. Freeman.* ABOVE: *The Union fleet passing forts Jackson and St. Phillip below New Orleans. Most noticeable is the ram CSS* Manassas *at the extreme right side of the engraving. In the center of the engraving, the USS* Hartford *is attacked by a fire raft on her port side.*

It took the better part of a month to get the entire Union fleet over the sandbars at the mouth of the Mississippi River. By the beginning of April the fleet was finally over the bar and in position to begin the reduction of New Orleans and its two forts. Porter's twenty-one mortar schooners were brought to within one mile (1.6km) of the forts and anchored. Their masts were camouflaged to reduce the potential for counterbattery fire. At 9:00 A.M. on April 18, Porter gave the order to open the mortar barrage on the forts. Each 13-inch (33cm) mortar fired one round every ten minutes; and more than three thousand mortar rounds were fired over the course of ten hours.

At nightfall, Farragut called a cease-fire and sent a small force forward to assess damage. The team found the forts on fire, but realized that a long period of siege would be necessary to reduce them. The next day, with ammunition running short, Farragut slowed the mortar schooners' rate of fire to two rounds every hour.

A bird's-eye view of the Union fleet passing the forts below New Orleans.

If Farragut was to run the river past the forts and get above them, the chain and hulk blockade had to be dealt with. He ordered a couple of gunboats to attempt a breach of the blockade with electrically detonated explosives. Intense Confederate artillery fire from the two forts prevented the explosives from being set, but sweat, axes, and saws accomplished the desired end, and the blockade was breached sufficiently on the eastern side of the river to allow the fleet to pass.

The Confederate naval forces, led by Commander John K. Mitchell, were augmented by the Confederate Army's River Defense Fleet, which remained independent from the navy, and the Louisiana State Navy, which was completely independent. Mitchell, in disagreement with the Confederate ground commander, Brigadier General Johnson Duncan, kept the majority of his fleet north of the hulk blockade and out of mortar range. The Confederate fleet, consisting of

several ironclads and other river steamers, would await the Union fleet north of the blockade line and attack it as it attempted to move upstream against the river current and around the bend at the forts. It was decided that each individual Confederate ship captain would make his own decisions in the upcoming battle.

Farragut's plan called for his fleet, which was divided into three sections (red, blue, and red-blue), to run past the forts in that

Farragut brought Union mortar boats up to bombard Fort Jackson before attempting to pass it with the fleet. The masts were camouflaged with trees to help conceal the mortar boats from Confederate observers directing counterbattery fire.

Union Captain Theodorus Bailey and Lieutenant George H. Stevens on their way to the city hall to accept the surrender of New Orleans. Confederate forces had evacuated the city to prevent its destruction, leaving its citizens at the mercy of the occupying Federal troops.

order, negotiate the breached hulk blockade, and fight the Confederate ships above the forts. The red segment, commanded by Captain Theodorus Bailey, consisted of the USS *Cayuga,* the USS *Pensacola,* the USS *Mississippi,* the USS *Varuna,* the USS *Oneida,* and three gunboats. The blue segment, commanded by Farragut, would consist of the heavy frigates USS *Hartford,* USS *Brooklyn,* and USS *Richmond.* The final red-blue segment, commanded by Captain Henry Bell, was composed of the USS *Iroquois* and five gunboats.

In the early morning hours of April 23, the fleet set off in order up the river. The night was pitch black as the fleet approached the forts and began the battle. Although raked by heavy fire from the forts, the van-guard red segment negotiated the hulk

blockade and was the first to come into contact with the Confederate fleet. The iron-clad ram CSS *Manassas,* commanded by Lieutenant A.F. Warley, surged among the wooden Union ships, but was sunk after ramming only two of them and inflicting serious, though not fatal, damage. The CSS *Governor Moore,* with Lieutenant Beverly Kennon commanding, managed to ram and sink the USS *Varuna* before being so badly shot up that, like many others, the boat had to be burned to prevent her capture.

Ship by ship, the Union fleet negotiated the forts, the hulk blockade, and the Confederate Navy. The death toll was high and the damage significant, but the fleet finally got past the forts. Ships stopped for their crews to repair them, bury the dead, wash the gore from the decks, and prepare for the next engagement: taking the city of New Orleans. On April 25, Union troops entered New Orleans and reoccupied the Federal buildings. On May 1, all hostilities in New Orleans were brought to an end with the formal surrender of the remaining Confederate land and naval forces in the city.

ISLAND NUMBER 10 AND MEMPHIS, TENNESSEE

Between the confluence of the Ohio and Mississippi Rivers at Cairo, Illinois, and the mouth of the Mississippi River below New Orleans, there are a number of islands. During the Civil War, these islands were numbered consecutively from Cairo to New Orleans. In the bend of the Mississippi River near New Madrid, Missouri, was Island Number 10. The Confederates had made this choke point in the river into a formidable fort, defended by seventy-five cannon and six thousand troops.

At the same time that Farragut was approaching New Orleans, the Mississippi

TOP: The sloop of war USS **Brooklyn.** *Commissioned just before the war, in 1859, the* **Brooklyn** *fought in every major engagement in the West. She continued to serve in the U.S. Navy until 1889, when she was decommissioned and sold. ABOVE: The Union fleet attacks Fort St. Phillip below New Orleans.*

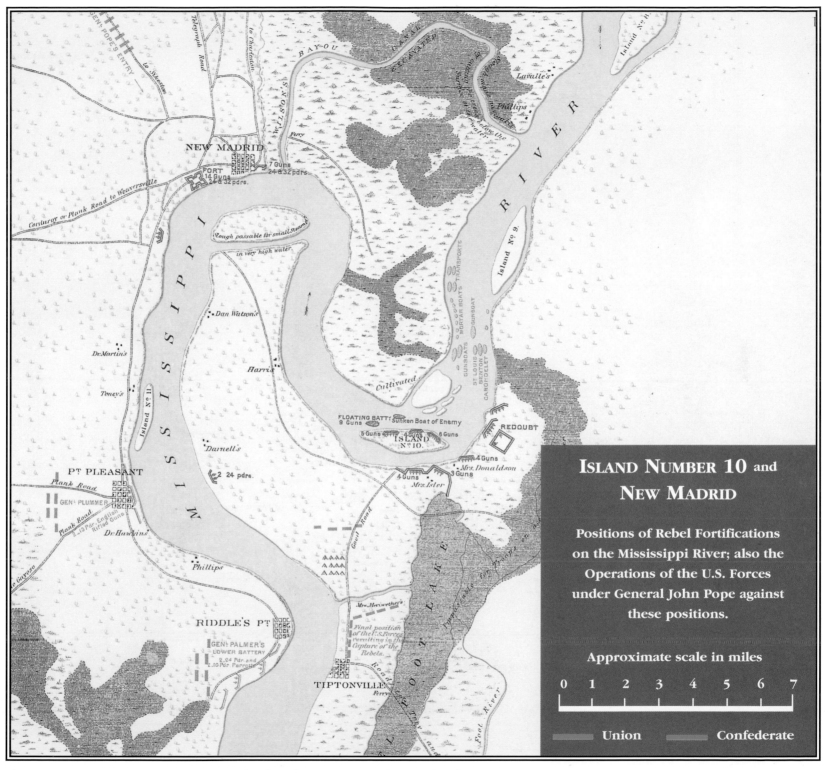

Map labels (as printed on the map):

GEN! POPE'S ENTRY
to Sikeston
Telegraph Road
to Charleston
BAYOU
WILSON'S
CANAL EXCAVATED
RIVER
Island No. 8
Lavalle's
Phillips
NEW MADRID
FORT 14 Guns 24 & 32 pdrs.
7 Guns 24 & 32 pdrs.
Ferry
Corduroy or Plank Road to Weaversville
Rough passable for small Steamers in very high water
below the water
Island No. 9
MISSISSIPPI
Dan Watson's
MORTAR BOATS TRANSPORTS
GUNBOAT
GUNBOATS
ST LOUIS BENTON CARONDELET
Dr.Martin's
Harris'
Toney's
Cultivated
Island No. 11
FLOATING BATT'Y 9 Guns   Sunken Boat of Enemy
5 Guns   6 Guns
ISLAND N°. 10.
REDOUBT
Darnell's
4 Guns
Mrs. Donaldson
2 24 pdrs.
4 Guns   3 Guns
Mrs. Isler
PT PLEASANT
Plank Road
GEN! PLUMMER
Plank Road
2 10 Pdr. English Rifled Guns
Dr.Hawkins
Good Road
to Gayoso
Phillips
REELFOOT LAKE
Impassable for Troops &c.
RIDDLE'S PT
Mrs. Meriwether's
Final position of the U.S. Forces resulting in the Capture of the Rebels.
GEN! PALMER'S LOWER BATTERY
2 24 Pdr. and 2 10 Pdr. Parrotts
TIPTONVILLE
Ferry
Road to Troy and Fort... River

ISLAND NUMBER 10 and **NEW MADRID**

Positions of Rebel Fortifications on the Mississippi River; also the Operations of the U.S. Forces under General John Pope against these positions.

Approximate scale in miles

0 1 2 3 4 5 6 7

Union   Confederate

This contemporary map of the area around Island Number 10 shows Confederate fortifications.

NAVAL WAR IN THE WEST

LEFT: During a violent thunderstorm on the night of April 1, 1862, a handpicked raiding party of forty men from the 42nd Illinois Regiment assaulted the upper battery at Island Number 10 and spiked the Confederate cannon there, making them useless to oppose the passage of the Union fleet. ABOVE: On June 6, 1862, the citizens of Memphis, Tennessee, watched as the Union fleet completely destroyed what was left of the Confederates' Mississippi River Defense Fleet. The way to the key city of Vicksburg, Mississippi, was now open.

River Fleet, with Foote commanding, was anchored off Island Number 10. In early March, U.S. Army General John Pope attacked and seized New Madrid with twenty-five thousand infantrymen. If the Union Navy could get some gunboats past Island Number 10, Pope's infantry would be able to cross the river and invest Island Number 10 from the south.

On April 4, Walke, commanding the USS *Carondelet,* volunteered to run the gauntlet past Island Number 10. On a pitch-black night, the specially prepared boat began its secret passage. A sudden thunderstorm lit up the night as the boat slid past the Confederate batteries. To make matters worse, the coal dust residue in the *Carondelet*'s stacks caught fire and lit up the boat. Confederate batteries opened up, but to no avail. The *Carondelet* was safely past. The

feat was duplicated on April 6 by the USS *Pittsburg.* On April 7, without delay, the two gunboats patrolled while Pope's infantry crossed the river and landed below Island Number 10. By late afternoon the fort had surrendered, and the Mississippi river was open all the way to Memphis, Tennessee.

North of the key port of Vicksburg, the only remaining Confederate stronghold was Memphis. The Mississippi River Fleet, accompanied by Pope and his infantry, eased down the river, anchored at Plum Point, and began their usual mortar bombardment of Fort Pillow, north of Memphis. Captain Charles Davis replaced the injured Captain Foote on May 9. On May 10, the USS *Cincinnati* deposited a mortar scow at the bank and anchored nearby, steam down. Suddenly, eight ships appeared steaming up the river. They were cottonclad rams of

*The USS **Pittsburg**, one of the city-class Eads ironclads.*

the Confederate Army's Mississippi River Defense Fleet, commanded by Commodore James Montgomery and his companion, General Jeff Thompson, a Missouri guerrilla leader.

The *Cincinnati*'s crew tried desperately to get her steam up, but she was struck almost instantly by the CSS *General Bragg*. Within a few minutes she was struck twice more by the CSS *Sumter* (not the raider of the same name) and the CSS *General Sterling*

Price. The *Cincinnati*'s 32-pounder (14.5kg) smoothbores blew holes through the lightly clad rams as she filled with water and sank to the bottom.

Nearby, the Union gunboats *Carondelet* and *Mound City* heard the cannon fire and steamed toward the action. The rebel steamer CSS *General Van Dorn* rammed and sank the *Mound City*. The *Carondelet* fired a 5-inch (12.7cm) Dahlgren rifle round through the CSS *Sumter*'s boilers, blowing her up. Sam

Phelps, commanding the USS *Benton*, fired an 8-inch (20.3cm) shell through the CSS *General Lovell*, hitting her boilers. He then turned on the CSS *General Van Dorn*, hitting her boilers as well. With the arrival of the heavy gunboats, the lightly armed Confederate River Defense Fleet broke off the engagement and headed south to the protection of Fort Pillow's guns. For the first time on the river, the Union fleet had been severely bloodied by Confederate naval forces.

TOP and BOTTOM: Two different artists' renditions of the battle before Memphis between Walke's fleet and Montgomery's Mississippi River Defense Fleet, June 6, 1862.

On May 25, Colonel Charles Ellet arrived with seven rams of the U.S. Army's Mississippi Ram Fleet, an organization completely independent of the navy. The vessels were designed for the specific purpose of ramming, and initially carried no armor or weapons. Later in the war they were armed with light cannon. On May 30, Confederate forces were forced to abandon Fort Pillow, blowing it up before withdrawing to Memphis.

Memphis was virtually defenseless. These men and boats that could be spared had been sent to defend New Orleans. The entire garrison at Memphis consisted of about two hundred troops and the eight ships that remained of Commodore Montgomery's River Defense Fleet after the fight on May 10.

In the predawn hours of June 6, the Union Navy came to Memphis. Montgomery's eight ships stood across the river in two lines abreast. Ellet's rams competed with Davis' ironclads for the honor of reaching the Confederate fleet first. In the smoky dawn, the Union rams and gunboats destroyed Montgomery's fleet with virtually no losses of their own. Only the CSS *General Van Dorn* managed to escape destruction and run to Vicksburg. At 11:00 A.M. that same day, Union troops landed unopposed and took control of Memphis.

chapter 3

1862
NAVAL WAR IN THE EAST

THE *MONITOR* AND THE *MERRIMACK*

By all rights, the battle between the USS *Monitor* and the CSS *Virginia* should never have taken place. Neither ship was ready for battle, and both ships barely made it to Hampton Roads that fateful day.

The CSS *Virginia* was built using the hull of the former USS *Merrimack*, which had been burned at Norfolk when the Union forces evacuated. Although officially named the CSS *Virginia*, the ship is almost always referred to as the *Merrimack*. Confederate Secretary of the Navy Mallory asked for designs for an ironclad ship capable of at least coastal water operation. After some discussion, a design conceived by noted ordnance expert Lieutenant John Mercer Brooke, based on the hull of the *Merrimack,* was selected. The novelty in Brooke's design was that the armor on the *Merrimack* would extend below the waterline, with the decks awash. One great flaw, however, was that her anchor and screw were exposed and vulnerable to ramming or cannon fire. Naval Constructor John L. Porter and Engineer-in-Chief William P. Williamson were directed to build the ship, while Brooke was made responsible for her armor and weapons.

In spite of delays, changes, material shortages, lost shipments, strikes, and the other problems usually associated with government contracts, the *Merrimack*, using her flawed original steam engines, was finally launched on February 13, 1862. Brooke had altered his designs so that the vessel now had a casemate of twenty-four inches (60.9cm) of pine and oak planking, and four

PAGE 63: *A somewhat fanciful depiction of the battle between the USS* Monitor *and the CSS* Virginia. *On the left, the USS* Cumberland *sinks. ABOVE: Tom W. Freeman's painting of the CSS* Virginia, *the ironclad built on the recovered bulk of the USS* Merrimack, *in drydock. There are no known photographs of the* Virginia, *but several contemporary drawings survive.*

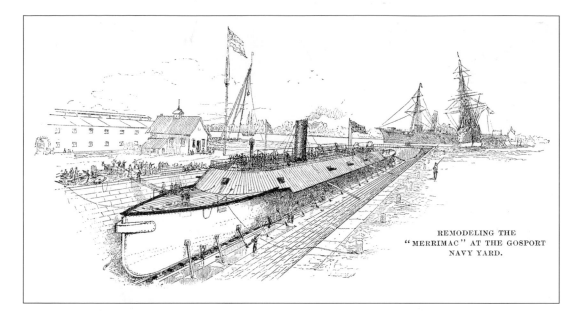

REMODELING THE "MERRIMAC" AT THE GOSPORT NAVY YARD.

TOP: A contemporary drawing of the CSS Virginia in drydock at Gosport Navy Yard, Norfolk, Virginia. ABOVE: Two Union naval officers survey the damage to the Monitor's turret caused by gunfire from the Virginia. Note the two large dents in the turret to the left of the left-hand gunport.

inches (10.1cm) of iron plate. The casemate was open to the sky and covered with a grating of two-inch (5cm) iron bars, leaving it highly vulnerable to plunging fire.

Brooke armed the *Merrimack* with two 7-inch (17.7cm) rifles fore and aft, 6.4-inch (16.2) rifles at the forward corner ports, and six 9-inch (22.8cm) Dahlgren smoothbores, three on each side. To complete her armament, a two-foot-long (0.6m), fifteen-hundred-pound (681kg) iron ram was affixed to her bow. She was now the most dangerous warship afloat. One major disadvantage, however, was that she had a twenty-three-foot (7m) draft, very deep for inland waters. Her draft was made deeper by the fact that two hundred tons (181.6t) of pig iron had to be put in the bilges to keep the boat upright in the water. By the time a full complement of ammunition and one hundred fifty tons (136.2t) of coal were on board, she wallowed, and was barely steerable at her top speed of nine knots (4.6 m/sec).

To crew the *Merrimack*, a call was sent out for volunteers, and a few trained seamen were found. The rest of the crew, some two hundred men, were taken from a nearby infantry unit. Mallory personally selected Captain Franklin "Old Buck" Buchanan to command the ship, with Lieutenant Catesby Ap. R. Jones as his executive officer. Mallory's orders to Buchanan were simple: steam into Hampton Roads, sink the Union vessels there, and break the blockade.

At the same time that the Confederacy was rebuilding the *Merrimack* as an ironclad, the Union navy was seeking its own design for a series of ironclad ships. Secretary of the Navy Gideon Welles asked for plans for an ironclad vessel. Initially, two designs were submitted. The first, by Cornelius Bushnell, was for an armored ship to be called the USS *Galena,* while the second, by Merrick & Sons of Philadelphia, was for a wood-framed steam frigate with an iron casemate, to be

OPPOSITE: Port side of the experimental ironclad USS Galena *looking forward. An early experiment in ironclad design, the* Galena's *armor failed when struck at right angles by plunging fire. The armor was removed in 1863, when the* Galena *was converted to a three-masted screw sloop. ABOVE: Officers of the USS* Monitor *pose for a group photograph before the famous battle against the CSS* Virginia.

Captain John Worden commanded the USS Monitor. Worden was severely wounded during the battle when a round from the CSS Virginia struck the pilothouse and blinded him.

Captain Franklin "Old Buck" Buchanan, commander of the CSS Virginia, was a longtime U.S. Navy officer who resigned his commission in order to serve his native state of Virginia.

called the USS *New Ironsides*. Welles' board asked Bushnell to submit some guarantees that his design for the *Galena* would actually float and move. Bushnell sought the advice of John Ericsson, an eccentric but distinguished boatbuilder. Ericsson told Bushnell that the *Galena* design would indeed work, and he asked Bushnell to take a look at his own design for an iron ship. Ericsson's design had previously been submitted to Napoleon III of France, but had been dropped when the Crimean War ended. The design was for an armored flat raft with a rotating cupola on top. One large gun mounted in the rotating cupola would be able to fire in any direction.

Impressed by Ericsson's plans, Bushnell took them to Welles, who was also captivated by the novel idea of the turret. The turret

was to become a standard element in the design of naval men-of-war for the next hundred years, but the board was still not convinced. Certain that Ericsson's was the best design, Welles and Bushnell convinced President Lincoln to support the plan. In a final showdown, Ericsson, backed by Welles and Lincoln, appeared before the board. The board finally acted, deciding that all three designs would be built: the *Galena*, the *New Ironsides*, and Ericsson's *Monitor*.

The *Monitor* was 172 feet (52.4m) long and forty feet (12.1m) wide, and had a draft of ten feet (3m). She had a wooden hull below the waterline, and her overhanging deck, five inches (12.7cm) above the waterline, was a twenty-six-inch (66cm) layer of white oak covered with five inches (12.7cm) of laminated iron plate. The turret was a

massive metal can, nine feet high (2.7m) and twenty feet (6m) in diameter, made of eight-inch-thick (20.3cm) laminated iron plate except at the gunports, where the turret was protected with an extra inch (2.5cm) of iron plate. The structure was open at the top, with an iron grate across the opening. It sat on the raft, held down by its own weight, and it was arranged so that it could be lifted from the deck slightly and rotated with the use of gears driven by a separate engine. In trial runs, it was found that the small steam engine could turn the turret two and a half revolutions per minute. Ericsson asked for two guns to be mounted in the turret side by side, and was given two 11-inch (27.9cm) Dahlgren smoothbores capable of firing 166-pound (75.3kg) shot.

Ericsson's design incorporated several novel features besides the turret. The anchor was enclosed in a recess in the bow of the ship, allowing it to be raised or lowered under fire without exposing the crew. There were two steam engines running a single drive shaft that turned a four-bladed screw nine feet (2.7m) in diameter. The screw was protected underwater by the boat's armored stern. The engines' boilers drew air through two shafts which terminated flush with the deck. These shafts were connected to two giant belt-driven blowers which, at least in theory, would move fresh air into the engine and living compartments while exhausting toxic, stale air from the ship. The pilothouse was on the front of the bow, preventing the *Monitor*'s guns from firing directly forward.

On January 30, 1862, the *Monitor* slid down the ways at the Continental Iron Works in New York City and, to the amazement of some, she floated. Several more weeks of finishing work were required, and her newly named commander, Lieutenant John L. Worden, went about gathering a crew. By February 19, the *Monitor* was ready to be turned over to Worden. He fired up her boil-

Abraham Lincoln meeting with civilian and military leaders aboard the U.S. revenue steamer **Miami.**

the threat to the fleet in Hampton Roads was real, and the Union needed the *Monitor* there as soon as possible to deal with the threat from the *Merrimack*.

On March 6, the *Monitor*, pulled by a tug, the *Seth Low*, and accompanied by two gunboats, the *Currituck* and the *Sachem*, steamed down the East River and into the Atlantic Ocean. For some unknown reason, Welles cabled the naval commander and ordered the *Monitor* to come directly to Washington instead of Hampton Roads. Fortunately, the *Monitor* had already sailed.

On March 7, on the open ocean, the *Monitor* was hit by a major storm. Seawater came over her two-foot (0.6m) freeboard and cascaded down the air ventilator shafts, fouling the blowers and killing the boiler. Without the blowers, the crew spaces filled with noxious fumes, and crew members dropped unconscious. Topside, Worden attempted to signal the tug, but no signal flares were available and the tug paid no attention. Several efforts were made to get the pumps started and the blowers working, but to no avail. Luckily, the wind and waves died before the situation could become truly disastrous. The crew of the *Monitor* was able to repair the damage, and she was once again under way.

At Norfolk on March 6, Buchanan had planned to make his way out of the yard and into Hampton Roads during the night hours, arriving on station at daybreak. The pilot, however, would not run the river without channel lights, all of which had been removed by the Confederates as a precaution against invasion. On March 7, the pilot refused again to sail, as Norfolk was being buffeted the same storm that was battering the *Monitor* farther out to sea. Buchanan could only fume and wait.

March 8 dawned bright and clear. Buchanan ordered the *Merrimack* to head for Hampton Roads. As a final preparation for

ers and set out on the East River. Within a short time, however, one of her engines failed, and it took several hours to return the vessel to the docks for a week's repairs. Following the repairs, the *Monitor* was ordered out again, but this time it was found that she would not respond to the wheel. After careening rather comically around the river and running into the banks, she was returned once again to the docks. Finally, in testing the boat's two 11-inch (27.9cm) guns,

Worden discovered that they could only be fired one at a time because of the manner in which the gunport shutters were rigged.

In Washington, meanwhile, rumors were rampant concerning an imminent attack by the *Merrimack*. At one point, members of the White House staff panicked and ran to the windows to see if the *Merrimack* was coming up the Potomac River, only to be reminded that her draft was too deep to cross the bar several miles downriver. Still,

NAVAL WAR IN THE EAST

battle, her sides were covered with fat and tallow in the belief that it would make the cannon balls slide off more easily. The engineering officer confidently assured Buchanan that although the *Merrimack* had not had a shakedown cruise, the ten-hour trip down the river would serve the purpose well, providing the opportunity to identify problems and make any necessary repairs. The iron-clad boat steamed into the bay accompanied by two smaller boats, the *Raleigh* and the *Beaufort*. The Union fleet lay at anchor, stretched from Newport News around the end of the peninsula to Fortress Monroe. The U.S. Navy's largest men-of-war—the *Congress, Cumberland, Minnesota, St. Lawrence,* and *Roanoke*—watched in silence as the *Merrimack* lumbered slowly toward them. It was unthinkable that any ship could withstand the thirty-five-gun broadside from one of these huge ships. Yet the *Merrimack* came on, headed toward the *Congress*.

Aboard the *Congress*, the crew waited silently over their guns until the *Merrimack* was a mere one hundred yards (91.4m) away, point-blank range. Finally the *Congress* delivered a full broadside into the

OPPOSITE: On March 8, 1862, the Confederate ironclad CSS Virginia, *seemingly impervious to cannonfire, swept past the USS* Congress, *a frigate commissioned in 1842, and set her on fire. The* Congress *burned down to the waterline. Painting by Tom W. Freeman. ABOVE: The USS* Monitor *(left) and the CSS* Virginia *(right) move in close to fire at each other in the famous battle at Hampton Roads, Virginia, on March 9, 1862.*

Merrimack. As the smoke cleared, the *Congress*'s crew was amazed to see that the Confederate ship had suffered no damage at all. Lieutenant Jones then ordered the *Merrimack*'s starboard guns to fire, and the *Congress*'s wooden side was instantly blasted into kindling.

The *Merrimack* continued on, moving toward the *Cumberland*. Buchanan steamed in at an angle from which the *Cumberland*

ABOVE: Lieutenant W. N. Jeffers, the officer who took charge of the USS Monitor *during its battle with the CSS* Virginia *after Captain Worden was wounded, continued to command the* Monitor *through most of the rest of her short career. RIGHT: Another artistic rendition of the battle between the ironclads* Monitor *and* Virginia *at Hampton Roads.*

could not bring any of her twenty-two 9-inch (22.8cm) Dahlgrens or her 10-inch (25.4cm) pivot gun to bear. He fired one round from a forward 7-inch (17.7cm) rifle, which exploded among the *Cumberland*'s contingent of marines, killing and wounding several of them. The *Merrimack* then rammed the *Cumberland* at full speed, striking her just behind the bow and tearing a hole in the hull below the waterline. Instantly, the *Cumberland* fired a point-blank broadside into the *Merrimack*. The *Merrimack*'s ram was caught in the *Cumberland*'s side, giving the *Cumberland* the opportunity to blast the *Merrimack* with three more broadsides. The *Merrimack* at last showed some damage, and some of her crew were killed, but more importantly, the sinking *Cumberland* was threatening to pull the *Merrimack* down with her. Finally, however, the fifteen-hundred-pound (681kg) ram ripped itself from the bow of the *Cumberland,* and the *Merrimack* was able to back off.

While the *Merrimack* was engaged with the *Cumberland,* tugs began moving the remaining Union men-of-war into the fight. The *Minnesota*, the *St. Lawrence*, and the *Roanoke* were all run aground on the sandbars in the bay. Another tug came to the assistance of the *Congress*, now heavily damaged, and ran her aground as well. All of the Union ships were now helplessly stuck and could only await the fatal attack of the massive ironclad.

The *Merrimack* turned back to the *Congress* and began raking her with cannon fire. For two hours the *Congress* accepted the punishment, while making feeble attempts to return fire. With his crew nearly all wounded or killed, the acting captain of the *Congress*, Lieutenant Austin Pendergast, ordered the colors struck and white flags raised. The Confederate *Beaufort* was ordered to come alongside, remove the wounded, and burn the *Congress*. While she lay alongside, Union

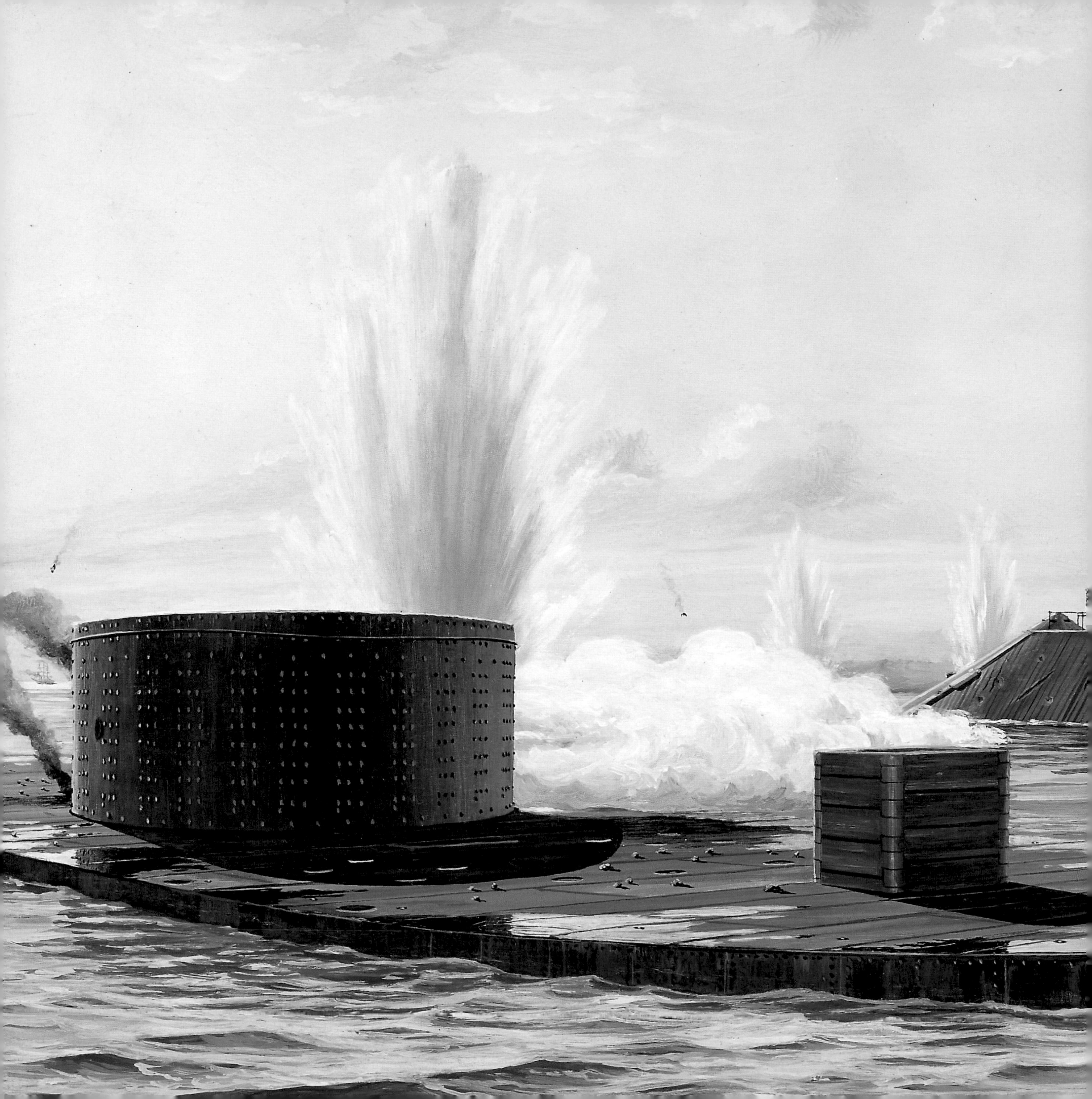

infantry and artillery, perhaps not understanding or seeing the surrender, opened up on the *Beaufort*, wounding many of her crew. This apparent violation of the law of naval warfare enraged many of the Confederate officers. The *Beaufort* pulled away out of range of the shore-based guns. Buchanan, standing on the deck of the *Merrimack* and firing a rifle at the *Congress*, was himself wounded by a rifle shot, and he had to turn command of the *Merrimack* over to Jones. Jones then fired repeated rounds of hot shot into the *Congress*, setting her ablaze.

It was about 5:00 P.M. now. Jones wanted to finish off the *Minnesota* before steaming to rest under the protection of Confederate guns at Sewell's Point for the night. But it was getting late, and he did not want to risk running aground in the dark. The *Merrimack* had taken a few good hits from the *Cumberland*. She was leaking a little water, a couple of her guns had been disabled, and some of her crew, including Old Buck, had been wounded. Jones reasoned that the ships would all be there tomorrow, so he turned the *Merrimack* and headed for Sewell's Point.

During the night, the burning *Congress* served as a beacon and a notice of what the next day might hold for the U.S. fleet. Around midnight, the watching Confederates saw the chugging form of a boat, but it was a boat unlike any they had seen before. It looked like a water tank on a raft.

The *Monitor* had arrived at Hampton Roads too late to save the *Congress* or the *Cumberland*. Worden anchored the *Monitor*

and reported to the senior commander, Captain John Marston on the *Roanoke*. Marston's only order to Worden was to protect the *Minnesota* when the *Merrimack* came down, as she surely would the next morning. Worden steamed the *Monitor* to the wounded *Minnesota* and anchored next to her. Aboard the *Monitor*, the crew, without sleep or food, kept busy all night helping the *Minnesota*. The *Congress* finally exploded. Meanwhile, at Sewell's Point, after the wounded had been tended to and repairs to the *Merrimack* made, her crew slept and, on the following morning, ate a hearty breakfast.

At 6:00 A.M. the following day, March 9, 1862, the *Merrimack* fired a shell from one of her forward batteries into the battered *Minnesota*. Worden ordered the *Monitor's* crew to battle stations and began an indecisive engagement that would forever change naval warfare.

Worden decided to engage the *Merrimack* as far from the *Minnesota* as possible, hoping to keep her occupied and prevent an attack on the stranded, vulnerable wooden man-of-war. As the two iron ships closed in on each other, they began to steam in an ever-decreasing circle, until they were firing into each other at point-blank range. Suddenly, the *Merrimack*, whose draft was thirteen feet (3.9m) deeper than the *Monitor's*, ran hard aground on a sandbar. Jones ordered the engineer to lash down the engine's safety valves and get her off the sandbar or blow her up in the attempt. Everything that could burn was thrown into the furnace, increasing the boiler's pressure to dangerous levels, and the churning screw finally backed the boat off of the bar. Jones then ordered his crew to prepare to ram the *Monitor*.

Aboard the *Monitor*, Worden saw the boarding party forming on the *Merrimack's* hurricane deck. He ordered his men to prepare to repel boarders and to load the 11-

inch (27.9cm) Dahlgrens with canister shot. Worden's gunner reported that both guns were already charged with solid shot, and Worden ordered them fired. The first round struck the *Merrimack* hard and tore away some of her armor, but the second gun would not fire, having been improperly loaded. Worden ordered the *Monitor* into shallow water where the *Merrimack* could not follow, giving his gunners the fifteen minutes they needed to repair the gun. But the *Merrimack* gave chase and struck a glancing blow against the *Monitor*, doing more harm to herself than to the other ship. Nonetheless, the *Monitor* was able to get into the shallows and repair her gun, returning thereafter to continue to battle.

The two ironclads continued to rake each other. Aboard the *Monitor*, the gunnery officer could not see the *Merrimack* because of his enclosed position inside the turret, and he could not tell what direction he was pointed in. Moreover, the machinery used to rotate the turret had been damaged by seawater, so that the turret could not be stopped with any precision. The turret's guns had to be fired on the fly each time the turret rotated past the *Merrimack*.

Worden once again ran the *Monitor* into shallow water to replenish ammunition in the turret and conduct a damage check. He found the boat to be in good shape despite the intense fire from the *Merrimack*, so he ordered her off the shoal and back into the action. Within minutes, the two ships were hammering each other again. A shell from the *Merrimack* struck the pilothouse on the *Monitor*, blinding Worden and knocking down the others with him. Worden, not knowing the damage to his ship, ordered the helmsman to sheer off. As soon as the executive officer came on the scene, Worden put him in command and ordered him to save the *Minnesota*. In the confusion, however, the helmsman received no further orders and

This contemporary engraving shows the crew of the Monitor *abandoning ship as she founders in a gale off the coast of North Carolina on December 31, 1862. Her tug, the USS* Rhode Island, *is shown in the background.*

NAVAL WAR IN THE EAST

After the battle at Hampton Roads, Confederate fortunes in the Norfolk area took a turn for the worse. In order to prevent her capture by Union forces, the crew of the CSS Virginia *blew her up and burned her on May 11, 1862.*

NAVAL WAR IN THE EAST

continued to widen the gap between the two warships. Finally, the executive officer ordered the *Monitor* around and in pursuit of the *Merrimack*.

Jones saw the *Monitor* break off the engagement and head for the shallow waters. His men were tired and his ship had been battered heavily by the *Monitor*'s 11-inch (27.9cm) guns. Also, the tide was running out, and if he did not get to safer waters he would have to spend the night in the sound with the Union ships. He finally ordered the pilot to head for the Elizabeth River and Norfolk. The *Monitor* briefly gave chase, but declined to run up under the Confederate land-based guns. The first battle between ironclad ships was over.

During the next month the *Merrimack* came down three times to battle again with the *Monitor*. However, William Jeffers, now commanding the *Monitor*, was under orders not to engage the *Merrimack*, and he refused to bring her out from under the protection of the Union's land-based guns. The blockade was preserved, and the South's one chance to break it was now lost.

Union victories in the Peninsular Campaign made Norfolk untenable. With Norfolk lost, the *Merrimack* had no place to go. Finally, in May, she was intentionally run aground and burned.

After the success of the *Monitor*, the United States Navy ordered new monitors of the Passaic class. The Passaic-class monitors were larger and heavier than Ericsson's original *Monitor*. In addition, certain innovations had been made based on the *Monitor*'s experiences. The pilothouse was now atop the turret rather than sitting in front of it. Also, inside the turret there was now one 11-inch (27.9cm) and one 15-inch (38.1cm) gun, instead of the *Monitor*'s two 11-inch (27.9cm) guns. The first of the class, the USS *Passaic*, was launched in November 1862. Others would follow in short order.

The *Monitor*, meanwhile, saw her last action in May 1862. Accompanied by the USS *Galena*, she steamed up the James River to Drewry's Bluff. There a hot battle ensued. The fort blasted the two ships and the *Galena* was severely damaged. The *Monitor* could not sufficiently elevate her 11-inch (27.9cm) guns to fire into the fort and was worthless in the fray. The ships broke off the battle and retired downriver. The *Monitor* would not see action again.

In late December, she was ordered to Charleston, South Carolina, for bombardment and blockade duties. While she was under tow on the Atlantic Ocean, a storm came up and she sank along with sixteen of her crew.

The Union blockade was successful. The *Merrimack*'s failure to break it only heightened expectations that the South would soon be sealed off from the outside. Charleston was one of the few ports that posed any threat to the blockade. Blockade-runners came and went from Charleston. With ironclad monitors, the U.S. Navy thought, Charleston could be brought to her knees.

Admiral Samuel DuPont was pushed by Welles to take a fleet of ironclads, steam into Charleston Harbor past the forts, and demand

The crew of this Passaic-class monitor poses on deck after a battle. Before them is the ship's retreat gun, a small cannon used for ceremonial purposes. Note the pilothouse mounted on top of the turret, an innovation based on the **Monitor***'s experiences in its fight with the* **Virginia** *.*

The double-turret monitor USS Onandaga. The crew in the foreground are shown rowing one of the ship's cutters. The enlisted men wear infantry-style kepis, while the officers wear the popular straw boaters.

NAVAL WAR IN THE EAST

the surrender of the city under threat of naval bombardment. By early 1863, the U.S. Navy had a number of ironclads. The first post-*Monitor* ironclad, the USS *Passaic,* had finished her trials and was ready for action. She was followed in short order by the USS *Weehawken,* the USS *Nantucket,* the USS *Montauk,* and the USS *Patapsco.* These vessels, along with the oddly built USS *Keokuk,* the USS *New Ironsides,* the USS *Nahant,* and the USS *Catskill* steamed into Charleston Harbor on April 7, 1863.

Immediately, things began to go wrong for the Federal fleet. The lumbering ships milled around, uncertain about mines and shallows. Finally, they fell into a position and began firing on Fort Sumter. Over the next few hours, the Confederates would pour more than two thousand rounds of every kind imaginable into the grouped ironclads. For their part, the ironclads would manage to fire a total of about one hundred fifty rounds from their 11-inch (27.9cm) and 15-inch (38.1cm) guns. Without doing any damage to Fort Sumter, the monitors were collectively shot up so badly that several were forced to withdraw from the fray. The *Keokuk* was hit more than ninety times and ultimately sank.

As evening arrived DuPont withdrew his ships with the thought that he would try again the next day. That night, at a meeting of his captains, he found that they unanimously felt that to go against Charleston the next day would be disastrous and lead to the loss of the fleet. The test of *Monitor*-type ironclad against fort had finally taken place and had found the ironclads no match for carefully emplaced and protected fortress artillery.

TOP: This contemporary drawing shows the use of the monitor fleet against Confederate shore defenses at Charleston, South Carolina, late in the war. ABOVE: The single-turret monitor USS Canonicus receiving coal from a supply ship on the James River before the battle for Richmond, Virginia. The large ironclads required constant refueling with coal to ensure full power from the boilers.

NAVAL WAR IN THE EAST

chapter 4

1863–1864
THE CONFEDERACY DIVIDED
IN THE WEST

VICKSBURG, PORT HUDSON, AND ARKANSAS POST

By early 1863 only two Confederate strongholds, Vicksburg and Port Hudson, stood in the way of the Union's drive to cut the Confederacy in half and deprive it of the supplies, food, and men it got from the states west of the Mississippi River. Lincoln demanded that Vicksburg be taken at all costs. If Vicksburg fell, the reasoning went, Port Hudson would be easily invested and taken as well. The Union would then have complete control of the Mississippi River plus the Atlantic and Gulf coasts, and would quickly starve the Confederacy into submission.

But taking Vicksburg was not to be that easy. Farragut, following his victory at New Orleans in April 1862, was under strict orders from Welles to proceed to Vicksburg and take the city. In early May, Farragut ordered his ships upriver to Vicksburg, though he was not keen on taking deep-draft ocean vessels so far up a river. He was further dismayed that the army had given him only twelve hundred infantrymen with which to assault and occupy Vicksburg.

With Captain Samuel P. Lee in charge of the expedition, Farragut's ships sailed with army transports in tow to Vicksburg. On May 18, 1862, Lee, under a flag of truce, demanded the surrender of the city. He was firmly rebuffed by the Confederate commander, Martin L. Smith. Lee was stymied. The Union troops, commanded by Brigadier Thomas Williams, were sick with malaria, dysentery, and scurvy. The army had not supplied rations for the infantrymen, so the army troops were fed from navy rations, putting

"They came in contact with a torpedo made to explode by striking & which exploded and tore the boat fearfully."

—Confederate saboteur Zere McDaniel in a telegram to Mississippi governor John J. Pettus, December 14, 1862, reporting the sinking of the USS Cairo by a naval mine in the Yazoo River

In this contemporary drawing, Porter's fleet is shown running downriver past the Vicksburg batteries on April 16, 1863. Note that coal barges and other unarmored vessels are lashed for protection to the city-class ironclads on the side opposite the bluffs. The burning stacks of logs at left were ignited by Confederate soldiers on the opposite shore to backlight the ships for the gunners on the bluffs.

PAGE 83: When Union ships ventured up the southern rivers, they found it tough going. Trees, vermin, snakes, Confederate snipers, fires, and insect-borne diseases made the effort hazardous and miserable for the crews of the boats. Here, sailors from Admiral David Porter's flotilla on the Red River use a makeshift log raft to clear the channel. ABOVE: This is the earliest known photograph of ironclads in action. Taken by Confederate photographer George S. Cook from the parapet of Fort Sumter, it shows the monitors Weehawken, Montauk, *and* Passaic *as they fire on the Confederate batteries at Fort Moultrie.*

everyone on half rations. There was no hope that they could storm up the cliffs at Vicksburg, which measured two hundred to three hundred feet (60.9m–91.4m) high, and take the Confederate positions. In addition, some of the ships' guns could not elevate high enough to fire at the uppermost land batteries. Finally, on May 25, Farragut, sick with dysentery, arrived at Vicksburg. All of his commanders counseled against trying to take the city with so few boats and troops. Farragut agreed and, leaving a token force to blockade the river at that point, fell back to New Orleans. The first attempt to take Vicksburg had failed.

Lincoln and Welles were outraged. Lincoln sent new orders to Farragut demanding that he assault Vicksburg. Farragut

regrouped his ships and, with his infantry reinforced to a total strength of thirty-two hundred men, returned upriver to Vicksburg. Farragut also recalled Admiral David Porter and his fleet of mortar schooners, which had been blasting away at Mobile and Pensacola since the taking of New Orleans. With the mortar schooners present and his fleet at anchor below Vicksburg, Farragut began his bombardment of the town in late June.

Using a courier, Farragut notified Flag Officer Charles Davis, whose Mississippi River Fleet was now at Memphis, that Farragut would run the batteries at Vicksburg and join with Davis above the city. Davis replied that he would leave Memphis immediately with his fleet.

On June 28, 1862, Farragut's fleet began the run upriver past the Vicksburg batteries. Porter's mortar schooners opened fire from below the city, and the army artillery units,

now stationed across the river, added supporting fire. Farragut's plan was similar to his New Orleans one: he would run upriver in double columns with the men-of-war spaced so that the gunboats could fire between them. By midday, the fleet, less one or two ships that failed to make the run, was above Vicksburg. Yet Farragut knew that the exercise was futile. Without sufficient supporting infantry, the flotilla could do nothing to reduce Vicksburg. The Confederates had an estimated three thousand troops in heavily fortified positions atop the bluffs, and twelve thousand additional troops within a day's march of the city. To send Williams's thirty-two hundred men against them would just result in pointless slaughter.

On July 1, Davis and the Western Gunboat Flotilla arrived at Farragut's position north of Vicksburg. The whole western navy was now assembled there: Davis' gunboats,

Commander Isaac N. Brown, C.S.N., a former U.S. Navy officer, joined the Confederate Navy at the war's beginning. In one of the most daring episodes of the war, he steamed the ironclad ram CSS Arkansas through the entire Union fleet at Vicksburg.

Ellet's rams, and Farragut's fleet. But with insufficient infantry support, the massed fleet could still do nothing. What was more, the river was falling, and Farragut knew that he had to get below Vicksburg before the water became too shallow for his men-of-war. Staying where he was ordered, he cabled Washington for instructions, noting the fact that if he did not move soon his blue-water fleet would be stuck in the Mississippi River until next year. Finally, Welles relented. He ordered Farragut and his fleet to the Gulf of Mexico, and ordered Davis and the gunboat flotilla to remain at Vicksburg and continue the assault.

Unbeknownst to the Union, the Confederate Navy was preparing a problem for the Union fleet. At Yazoo City, Mississippi, Commander Isaac Newton Brown, C.S.N.,

was completing the construction of the iron-clad ram CSS *Arkansas*, after she had been saved from destruction upriver after the fall of Memphis. Brown, an able commander for-merly of the U.S. Navy, was one of the Confederacy's senior officers. Brown scavenged iron and timber from every source imaginable to make the *Arkansas* impreg-nable against the Union ironclads. He gath-ered a crew from Confederate ships that had been destroyed. He assembled a motley group of cannon and built carriages for them. There was not enough armor to cover the whole boat, so portions of the ship, such as the pilothouse and stern, were left unar-mored. Finally, in mid-July, Brown, eager for combat, started the incomplete *Arkansas* down the Yazoo River toward the Mississippi.

During the trip down, the steam boxes leaked steam into the magazine and got the gunpowder wet. Brown stopped the boat

and had the crew take all the wet gunpow-der onto the river bank and dry it in the hot summer sun. By evening, the powder was dry and back aboard the boat. From time to time during the trip, Brown stopped along the riverbank to gather intelligence about possible Union naval activity. He was told that the Union fleet was still in the Mississippi above Vicksburg. What Brown did not know was that Farragut had ordered three Union boats—the ironclad *Carondelet* and the tinclads *Queen of the West* and *Tyler*—on a reconnaissance mission up the Yazoo that very day. Farragut knew that the *Arkansas* existed, but he believed that she would never appear, and that she did not pose a threat.

In the early morning hours of July 15, 1862, the *Arkansas* ran into the three Union ships. Immediately, the *Arkansas* opened fire on the ironclad and the two tinclads with her

The CSS Arkansas under construction at Yazoo City, Mississippi.

THE CONFEDERACY DIVIDED IN THE WEST

This painting by Tom W. Freeman depicts the CSS Arkansas *running among the Union fleet lying at anchor in the Mississippi River above Vicksburg on July 15, 1862. She deliberately came in very close to the Union men-of-war so as to prevent them from getting up to ramming speed.*

A contemporary photograph of the timberclad USS Tyler *lying at anchor. The timberclads were converted sidewheel towboats with a very light armoring of wood. Timberclads had a very shallow draft and made good reconnaissance vessels in the shallow waters of the western rivers.*

forward rifles. Initially, the Union ships tried to fight bow-on against the oncoming ram, but the commanders soon realized that they were no match for the Confederate ironclad. Captain Walke, aboard the *Carondelet,* ordered the ships turned back toward the Mississippi. But fire from the *Arkansas* cut into the ironclad, severing her steering gear. The *Carondelet* drifted into shallow water and received another broadside from the *Arkansas.* Seeing the ironclad disabled, Brown turned the *Arkansas* toward the two tinclads, which were waiting in the river to see the outcome of the ironclad battle.

The *Tyler* and the *Queen of the West* turned and fled toward the Mississippi and the security of the Union fleet. Brown had been wounded and his pilot killed by a shot

from the *Carondelet,* but he remained at his post. Fire from the *Tyler's* stern guns had no effect on the *Arkansas's* armor, but did damage the smokestack to the point where the boiler fires would barely draw. This served to cut the *Arkansas's* speed to almost nothing and nullify her ramming ability.

In the Mississippi, the Union sailors heard the firing and thought the three-ship force was firing on Confederate guerrillas along the bank. Within minutes, however, they observed the *Queen of the West* and the *Tyler* steaming toward them at full speed. Behind them, the *Arkansas* limped along slowly, belching cannon fire. The fleet was caught completely unprepared, its crews asleep and its boilers cold. Watch officers beat to quarters and, though immobile, the

fleet opened fire on the *Arkansas* with every gun available.

For half an hour, the *Arkansas*, with almost no motive power besides the river current, drifted among the Union ships, trading shots with the most powerful fleet on earth. Round after round cut into the *Arkansas*, peeling off the armor plate and riddling her with holes. Floating among the unmoving Union fleet, the *Arkansas* could fire all her guns as rapidly as possible. Finally, she cleared the fleet and drifted under the guns on Vicksburg's bluffs. Brown was given a hero's welcome.

Farragut was beside himself with anger. His repeated insistence that the *Arkansas* would never appear was recalled silently, if not out loud, by everyone in his command.

Ironclad ships were not invincible. In this depiction of action in February 1863 on the Mississippi River, the CSS Queen of the West, *a former Union ram captured and used by the Confederates, attacks the city-class ironclad USS* Indianola. *With the help of two other vessels, the ram CSS* William H. Webb *and the cottonclad CSS* Beatty, *the* Queen of the West *forced the ironclad to run aground. Her crew abandoned her, and she was burned by the Confederates the following day to prevent her recapture. Painting by Tom W. Freeman.*

He became a man possessed, and ordered an attack on the *Arkansas* that afternoon. But by the time he got the *Hartford, Sciota, Sumter* (salvaged by the Union Navy), and *Winona* under way it was dark, and the ships passed Vicksburg without sighting the *Arkansas* laid up at the wharf. The following day, Farragut conferred with Davis. Farragut wanted a combined daylight assault on the *Arkansas* using both fleets. Davis declined, fearing that

he might be caught below Vicksburg, cut off from his base at Memphis. An alternate plan was agreed upon.

Davis moved three of his gunboats to the bend in the river and began to fire upon the Vicksburg batteries with those boats and with his mortar scows anchored to their rear. Davis then sent the *Essex* and the *Queen of the West* toward the *Arkansas*, while Farragut sent the former Confederate ram *Sumter* up

to her. As the *Essex* closed in, the fire from her 10-inch (25.4cm) forward cannon tore into the *Arkansas*. With Brown unavailable for duty and only forty-one men capable of manning battle stations, the *Arkansas* continued to fight. One lucky 10-inch (25.4cm) shell from the *Essex* killed or wounded half the crew when it entered a gunport.

The *Essex* attempted to ram the *Arkansas*, but struck only a glancing blow and ran into the bank. The *Sumter* then ran in and struck the *Arkansas* broadside, but did little damage. The *Queen of the West* made the final ramming attack, but lost speed in maneuvering and also did little damage. All three ships were riddled by cannon fire from the bank and drifted away from the *Arkansas,* which remained defiantly afloat.

On July 24, Farragut finally turned south with his fleet and headed for the Gulf of Mexico and New Orleans. Davis took his gunboat flotilla and fell back all the way to Memphis. Vicksburg had once again proved to be too much for the Union Navy to take.

After a long, hot, and very difficult summer, Lincoln was perplexed by the fact that Vicksburg still stood. He ordered a political appointee, General John McClernand, to raise a force of men and take Vicksburg by land. Generals Grant and Sherman feared the intervention of the inexperienced McClernand, who was senior to Sherman. They conspired with Admiral David Porter, who had replaced Davis and was now commanding the western gunboat fleet, to beat McClernand to the punch. Their plan was simple: Grant would move down the Mississippi and engage Lieutenant General Pemberton's troops north of Vicksburg. At the same time, the gunboat fleet and Sherman, with thirty thousand men, would take Vicksburg by storm. It was December 1862 before the force was fully assembled and ready to make the assault.

Before Grant could get very far, Confederate cavalry destroyed his lines of supply, and he was forced to fall back to protect them. Sherman and Porter, however, did not know this. They plowed down the Mississippi with the gunboat fleet and eighty-five troop transports. Part of the fleet had been stationed at the mouth of the Yazoo River in early December. These boats were under orders to conduct reconnaissance up the Yazoo to determine the location of Confederate forces and artillery. On December

12, a task force of five boats was moving in the vicinity of Haines' Bluff when one of them, the USS *Cairo*, ran over a mine and became the first warship ever to be sunk in combat by a submerged mine.

On December 27, 1862, Sherman ordered the transports on the Yazoo River to a point about eighteen miles (28.8km) upriver from Vicksburg. From there, his troops disembarked from the transports into a swamp. Four infantry divisions slogged through the swamp, dogged by Confederate snipers, for a day and a half. Finally, they arrived at the base of a two-hundred-foot (60.9m) bluff, now manned by close to twenty thousand Confederate troops. Valor alone was not enough to carry

TOP: A contemporary photograph of the giant ironclad USS Choctaw. *She weighed 1,004 tons (910.8t) and was 260 feet (79.2m) long. She was converted from a steamer according to plans by William D. Porter. Her armor and armament were too heavy for her hull, making her slow and difficult to maneuver. An experimental two-inch-thick (5.1cm) rubber armor was constructed on her forward casemate but proved to be useless. ABOVE: The city-class ironclad USS* Essex *was captained by William D. Porter, elder brother of Admiral David Porter. The structures on the bow are privies for the crew to use while the ship is docked. The* Essex *was the vessel that finally finished off the CSS* Arkansas.

THE CONFEDERACY DIVIDED IN THE WEST
90

LEFT: On December 12, 1862, the USS Cairo, a city-class ironclad on a reconnaissance mission up the Yazoo River with four other boats, hit a Confederate naval mine and sank to the bottom in twelve minutes, becoming the first man-of-war ever sunk by a mine in combat. Painting by William R. McGrath. ABOVE: In 1964, the USS Cairo was raised from the bottom of the Yazoo River by the National Park Service and placed, with its contents, on display at the Vicksburg National Military Park. Here the pilothouse of the Cairo sees the light of day for the first time in 102 years.

the day, and on December 30, Sherman, having suffered 1,776 casualties, ordered his men back to the transports. Sherman and Porter planned to move farther upriver to Haines' Bluff and make another assault there, but bad weather prevented their attack. In abject defeat, Sherman fell back down the Yazoo River and turned his command over to McClernand, who had arrived during the battle. The third attempt to take Vicksburg had failed.

McClernand and Sherman decided to make a quick effort to take another Confederate position, known as Fort Hindman or Arkansas Post, which sat on the Arkansas side of the river just above Vicksburg. Regrouping the gunboats and the infantry, they stormed the small fort and occupied it within a couple of hours.

By this time, Vicksburg had become a truly irritating thorn in the side of the Union.

Tom W. Freeman's painting of the USS Choctaw. *Note the narrow bow and wide stern, designed to help stabilize the unwieldy boat. Her 11-foot (3.4m) draft was unsuitable for very shallow waters.*

It symbolized the Confederacy's stubborn resistance to the Union's best military efforts. Beginning on May 18, 1863, Grant, determined not to fail again, invested Vicksburg from the south and east, laying a protracted siege to the garrison. On July 4, after enduring incredible hardships, the Confederate forces at Vicksburg finally surrendered the city. On that same day, at Gettysburg, Pennsylvania, General Robert E. Lee was withdrawing to the South after an epic, three-day battle that would later be considered the turning point of the war, the "high-water mark of the Confederacy." And on July 9, Port Hudson, completely surrounded after the fall of Vicksburg, surrendered. The Confederacy was now cut in half, denied the support of its western states.

THE RED RIVER CAMPAIGN: COMBINED OPERATIONS GO SOUR

The Red River winds slowly and tortuously from Shreveport, Louisiana, southeast across the state until it enters the Mississippi above Port Hudson. After the collapse of Vicksburg and Port Hudson, there was little of military value in Louisiana, and few military men thought it worth any effort. However, the conduct of any war is guided by politics, and this one was no exception. Two important political matters concerned the administration in Washington. First was the fact that Napoleon III had established a government in Mexico under Maximillian of Hapsburg. The Confederacy had lines of communication open to the French through Mexico, and there was some concern that a French incursion into Texas, with Confederate complicity, might create a problem requiring a significant diversion of resources. Perhaps more importantly, the blockade of the South had created

A great danger to deep-draft sailing vessels was becoming grounded in a river under the enemy's guns. On Friday, May 13, 1863, the USS Mississippi, an old side-wheel frigate that had served as Commodore Matthew Perry's flagship during the Mexican War, ran aground directly under the guns of Port Hudson, Louisiana. Her crew set her on fire and abandoned her. Her magazines later blew up, finishing her completely. Painting by Tom W. Freeman.

a shortage of cotton, causing prices to soar to about $400 a bale. The Red River ran directly through Louisiana's cotton country. A valuable crop of Confederate cotton lay on the ground ready to be harvested by anyone who could get to it. The twin aims of the

Red River Campaign were to establish a Union military presence in western Louisiana that could deter a French incursion, and to sieze the valuable cotton crop.

In February 1864, President Lincoln ordered General Nathaniel Banks to depart

New Orleans, with naval support from Admiral David Porter and his gunboats, ascend the Red River, and seize the western Confederate capitol at Shreveport. General Banks's plan was to move his infantry along the river roads and have the Union Navy,

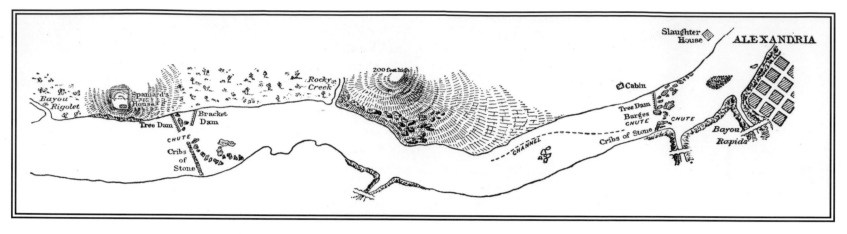

TOP: *In one of the most amazing engineering feats of the war, Union troops from Wisconsin constructed a dam to raise the Red River sufficiently so that the Union flotilla would not be trapped above the falls. This contemporary map shows the location of the dams above Alexandria, Louisiana.* ABOVE: *Once the dam was built and the water was high enough, each Union warship ran the chute over the falls to safety below. No ship was lost in the action.*

Porter released several vessels and their crews to scour the Louisiana countryside for cotton. They were accompanied by numerous speculators who had been given passes by President Lincoln, creating a climate of corruption and profiteering. More than two thousand bales of cotton were gathered and shipped to the military garrison at Cairo for auction. Meanwhile, however, Banks and his infantry continued to slog their way up the single roadway that paralleled the river, pulling ahead of Porter's fleet.

Porter could not get all of his boats past the falls north of Alexandria. He decided to establish a support base at Alexandria, and the *Eastport*, four ironclad gunboats, and a couple of tinclads were left to protect the site. By April 3, the task force had reached Grand Ecore. Here again certain vessels could not make the move upriver and were left behind to protect the lines of communication. Porter surged ahead with two monitors, the *Osage* and the *Neosho*, the tinclads *Cricket* and *Fort Hindman*, the timberclads *Lexington* and *Chillicothe*, and a string of transports carrying an infantry regiment from Sherman's army. The plan was to meet with Banks' force at a small landing located below Shreveport and coordinate their attack. But when Porter arrived at the designated meeting point, Banks' infantry was nowhere to be found.

with troop transports in tow, ascend the river. That way they would be able to trap any Confederate force they encountered in a pincer, crushed between Banks' infantry and Porter's gunboats.

The plan worked well on March 14, when the Union forces met their first resistance at Fort DeRussy. The gunboats fired into the fort, while the infantry attacked its weaker land side. The Confederate forces immediately withdrew northward, abandoning large quantities of weapons and stores. By March 16, Union troops occupied Alexandria, Louisiana. It was here that the seeds of disaster were sown.

General Nathaniel Banks, commander of Union forces during the Red River campaign to seize Shreveport, Louisiana, nearly brought on a disaster when he allowed his infantry to become separated from their supporting naval craft. The infantry became engaged with Confederate forces and the naval craft were left too far up the river. Only determination and luck prevented the entire task force from falling victim to the Confederates.

Late that afternoon, a runner advised Porter that Banks' force had been set upon and routed by Confederate forces at Sabine Crossroads, sixty miles (96km) to Porter's rear. Banks was in full retreat. Porter realized that he was now in a desperate position, where his flotilla could easily be cut off and destroyed piecemeal by Confederate land forces. He had to get out of the Red River as quickly as possible.

Porter turned around and made a dash for the south. All along the way, the fleet was under attack by Confederate forces. Several ships were damaged, abandoned, and blown up; others, including the *Osage*, ran

aground but were saved. Finally, after eight days of flight, Porter reached Grand Ecore. Gathering up the boats stationed at Grand Ecore, he then made a run for Alexandria.

In the ten days that it took to get from Grand Ecore to Alexandria, Porter's boats were constantly harassed by Confederate forces along the shore. Banks' retreat had left the Confederates unhampered in their efforts to slow and destroy Porter's fleet. The *Eastport* headed upriver to support the main fleet, but was lost when she ran aground and had to be blown up. The crews of several ships were killed by intense Confederate artillery fire. On April 28, Porter dragged into Alexandria to find his entire gunboat flotilla above the falls. The river was dropping rapidly, and as a result the falls had risen to four feet (1.2m), too high for many of the boats to go over safely. The Eads city-class ironclads *Carondelet, Mound City, Baron de Kalb,* and *Pittsburg,* the monitors *Osage* and *Neosho,* the *Chillicothe, Lexington, Ozark,* and assorted transports were all stranded.

With Confederate forces converging on him, Porter was in big trouble. As he contemplated the choice between surrender and a hopeless fight, an infantry officer, an engineer in civilian life, proposed creating a dam to raise the water and allow the boats to float over the falls. Despite the fact that the river was more than seven hundred feet (213.3m) wide, the dam, begun on May 2, was finished on May 8. By May 12, after many a heart-stopping moment, the entire fleet was over the falls and headed for safe waters.

The Red River expedition, an audacious plan driven more by economic and political concerns than by strategic considerations, was over. Despite the successful seizure of much valuable cotton, the mission was a dismal failure, and only ingenuity and a great deal of luck had kept it from becoming a total disaster.

A contemporary photograph of the Red River dam constructed above Alexandria, Louisiana, by Wisconsin troops.

chapter 5

1863–1864

Confederate Raiders on the Open Seas and the Final Forts

Confederate Commerce Raiders

Early in the war, Confederate Secretary of the Navy Mallory knew that his navy was at a serious disadvantage against the Union's naval forces. He had no ships of the line able to go toe to toe with the Union Navy. Instead, he decided to strike at the North's vulnerable mercantile fleet. It was a plan with several advantages: it would harm the North's economy by hampering trade with Europe; the Union would have to send men-of-war in pursuit of the Confederate commerce raiders, drawing resources away from the main fighting; the conflict would become more clearly international, and neutral European nations such as England and France would see that the Confederate States of America was more than a local insurrection; and, perhaps most importantly, the

"To act as a private armed vessel in the service of the Confederate States, on the high seas against the United States of America, their ships, vessels, goods and effects, and those of her citizens during the pendency of the war now existing."

—From the Letter of Marque authorizing the privateer Savannah, the first to be commissioned by the Confederate government

raiders could seize needed supplies and redirect them to the South.

Between June 1861, when the CSS *Sumter* steamed out of the Mississippi River, and November 1865, when the CSS *Shenandoah* surrendered in Liverpool, England, a series of Confederate commerce raiders brought U.S. oceangoing commerce to a virtual standstill. During that period, the major raiders, including the *Sumter, Florida, Alabama, Nashville, Shenandoah, Georgia, Tallahassee,* and *Chickamauga,* captured 211 commercial ships as prizes. Most prizes were emptied and burned. Several were paroled to return prisoners from captured ships. A few were recommissioned as Confederate raiders.

The first raider, the CSS *Sumter*, operated in the Caribbean Sea and in the Atlantic. Captained by Raphael Semmes, former U.S. Navy officer and lawyer, she took eighteen prizes in her relatively short career (June 1861 to January 1862). In truth, at 437 tons (396.8t), and with her small coal bunkers, the *Sumter* was too small and lacked the range to be truly effective as a raider. But by being the first raider on the high seas, she became a symbol of the threat posed by such raiders. As soon as she began taking prizes, foreign shippers stopped using U.S. carriers for their cargoes, and representatives of the merchant shipping industry besieged Washington with complaints. Some merchant ships sailed under foreign flags to reduce the danger of capture. Crews for the *Sumter* and other raiders were composed of foreign seamen, crews from prizes who enlisted after capture, and a few Confederate naval personnel.

As soon as Semmes reached Europe, he discovered the tangled labyrinth of diplomatic intrigue instigated by U.S. government representatives to the European nations. Depending on the political climate, Britain, France, and Spain supported or failed to support Confederate ships seeking refuge and repair in their harbors. Sometimes the law of

PAGE 97: Illustrating one of the great dangers of naval combat, this contemporary engraving shows a cannon exploding aboard the USS J.P. Jackson in Mobile Bay, Alabama. Explosions were caused by overloading, metal fatigue, and poor construction. RIGHT: The CSS Florida approaches a United States merchant ship to seize it as a prize. The general signal to heave to and surrender was a shot across the bow of the merchant ship. Painting by William R. McGrath.

neutrality was strictly adhered to, while at other times it was ignored. Sometimes provisions and coal could be obtained, other times not. When Semmes sailed into Gibraltar, a diplomatic storm ensued. Semmes knew that the *Sumter* was rotting and half her crew had deserted. So he sold the ship, paid off the remaining crew, and sailed to London, where he eventually took command of the CSS *Alabama.*

Of all the raiders, the *Alabama* was by far the most successful, bringing down sixty-nine prizes between August 1862 and her battle with the USS *Kearsage* in June 1864. The *Alabama* was one of several ships that the Confederate government obtained through their secret agent in England, Commander James Bulloch, C.S.N. Bulloch's mission was to obtain commerce raiders, built in England, for the Confederate Navy. However, Bulloch had to navigate around England's official neutrality and internal laws prohibiting such ventures. So, a diplomatic ruse was developed. The ship would ostensibly be built as a commercial vessel under British registration. Her armament would be purchased from other quarters and sent as freight aboard a second ship. When the ship was ready for sea, the two vessels would meet outside the territorial waters of any nation and the ship would be turned over to Confederate officers, commissioned in the Confederate Navy, and armed with the guns from the second ship. In this way Semmes obtained his second command. He enlisted

*The USS **Brooklyn** after the Civil War. Her funnel can be seen lowered just forward of the mainmast. She served the U.S. Navy until 1889.*

eighty-three foreign volunteers to serve as crew aboard the *Alabama*.

The *Alabama* operated throughout the sea lanes of the world, seizing and destroying U.S. merchantmen. In January 1863, Semmes sailed the *Alabama* to Galveston, Texas, only to find the city under fire from several Union warships. Semmes, flying the British ensign, lured one of the ships, the gunboat USS *Hatteras*, away from the protection of the other ships. When challenged,

Semmes ran down the British ensign and ran up the Confederate naval ensign. He fired a broadside into the *Hatteras* and got her to surrender before he burned her. Her crew was taken prisoner and transported to the island of Jamaica, where they were paroled.

The *Alabama* sailed the Caribbean, the Atlantic, the Cape of Good Hope, the Indian Ocean, and the Dutch East Indies taking prizes wherever she went. After two years afloat, she was in serious need of repair and

maintenance. Also, the crew was becoming dissatisfied with the long periods at sea and the declining numbers of prizes. In June 1864, Semmes steamed to the coast of France and docked at Cherbourg. Within a short period, the U.S. ambassador had cabled every U.S. station in Europe, notifying them that the *Alabama* was in Cherbourg. Off the coast of England, the USS *Kearsage*, under the command of Captain John Winslow (formerly a naval officer in the Mississippi

A clipper ship (foreground) lays on the sails to escape the CSS Alabama *(background) in hot pursuit.*

Kearsage, the crew was at Sunday services. They had watched the port for seven days without any activity, and were not expecting the *Alabama*. She was soon sighted, and the crew beat to quarters. Winslow decided that he would run the smaller, lighter *Alabama* down and ram her, but before he could do so, the *Alabama* opened fire. Soon the range was only five hundred yards (457.2m). Each ship held her rudder hard to starboard to prevent the other from having an opportunity for raking fire. This forced the two ships into a series of concentric circles, twisting around each other. The *Alabama*'s largest gun was a 7-inch (17.7cm) Blakeley rifle, while the *Kearsage* had two 11-inch (27.9cm) Dahlgrens and four 9-inch (22.8cm) Dahlgrens. As the range closed, the larger guns began to tell. Their massive charges ripped into the *Alabama*, killing several of her crew and disabling her engines. Finally, Semmes was forced to strike his colors. The surviving crew abandoned the sinking *Alabama*, and about half of them were picked up by several British and French pleasure craft that had observed the fight. These sailors, including Captain Semmes, were safely released in England, while the remainder were captured by the *Kearsage*.

Another of the British-built raiders, the CSS *Florida*, was commissioned in August 1862. She was placed under the command of Lieutenant John Maffit, C.S.N., who was only able to get about twenty men to enlist out of the one hundred twenty he needed to run the ship. Worse followed, however; as soon as Maffit took command, the ship's company was swept with yellow fever. Maffit had no surgeon and no medical supplies aboard. He realized that if he waited, he might lose the whole crew, including himself, to the disease. Maffit made directly for Mobile Bay, then under blockade by two Union ships. With only four hands well enough to man the ship, he ran the colors of the British Navy

Gunboat Flotilla), received the word and steamed for Cherbourg, where he anchored outside the harbor to await the *Alabama*.

Semmes was urged to avoid a fight with the Union man-of-war if possible. However, he determined to fight the *Kearsage*, and

announced his intention by issuing a challenge to the U.S. Consul in Le Havre through a Confederate agent there.

At midmorning on Sunday, June 19, 1864, Semmes steamed out of Cherbourg and straight for the *Kearsage*. Aboard the

LEFT: Tom W. Freeman's painting of the action between the CSS Alabama *(foreground) and the USS* Kearsage *off the coast of Cherbourg, France. ABOVE: This contemporary engraving depicts the gun-crew of the 11-inch (27.9cm) forward pivot gun of the* Kearsage *preparing to fire at the* Alabama*.*

until challenged, and then struck the British colors and made for the Mobile harbor. He easily outran the blockade ship and suffered only minor damage from gunfire. Once in Mobile, he recruited a crew sufficient to man the *Florida* properly.

Four months later, five days after the *Alabama* took the USS *Hatteras* off Galveston, Maffit and a fully crewed *Florida* shot out of Mobile Bay in the dark of the night and sped past the blockaders. The fact that the two most famous Confederate raiders were both roaming the high seas reflected badly on Secretary Welles, and in Washington there were calls for his resignation. Maffit roamed the Caribbean and the Atlantic at will, seizing

prizes. But after five continuous months at sea, the *Florida* was in dire need of overhaul. Maffit headed for the port of Brest, France.

In France, most of the enlisted crew deserted, and Maffit, weakened by his bout with yellow fever, was replaced by Lieutenant Charles Manigault Morris. In England, the Confederate agent Bulloch managed to enlist sixty men for her crew. By February 1864, she was ready to sail again and slipped into the Atlantic Ocean.

Morris ran up and down the Atlantic coast wreaking havoc among U.S. commercial vessels. Late in the year, he decided to head for the Pacific and attack the whaling

Commander Raphael Semmes, captain of the Alabama, *addresses his crew just prior to their engagement with the* Kearsage.

trade there. But on October 4 he first stopped in Bahia, Brazil, for overhaul and shore leave for the crew. The day following her entry into port, the USS *Wachusett*, a wooden screw sloop of ten guns, eased into port behind her. Two belligerents were now together in a neutral port. International law prescribed that only one vessel could leave within a twenty-four hour period. Thus, if the *Florida* left, the *Wachusett* would have to wait a day before pursuing her.

Commander Napoleon Collins of the *Wachusett* decided that the raider would never leave port. In a blatant violation of international law, Collins, in the dark morning hours of October 7, got a full head of steam and rammed directly into the starboard side of the *Florida*. Immediately, a boarding party from the *Wachusett* swarmed over the lightly manned *Florida* and took control. By that morning, the *Wachusett,* with the *Florida* in tow and under sail, left Bahia for the United States. Brazil was suitably outraged and demanded the return of the *Florida*, but the boat was improvidently sunk in an accident with an army transport ship a short time later. Collins was court-martialed

*The surrender team from the **Alabama** rows up to the **Kearsage** to announce the surrender and to request assistance for the Confederate crew of the sinking vessel.*

for the incident, but Welles declined to accept the verdict and sentence of the board, and Collins was allowed to retire some years later as an admiral.

The CSS *Tallahassee*'s career lasted a little over a month. Yet during that time she took thirty-eight prizes and successfully outran Union blockaders. After outfitting, this English-built ship ran from Wilmington, North Carolina, up the northeast coast. In August 1864, she put in at Halifax, Nova Scotia, for repair. The U.S. fleet attempted to bottle her up, but with the help of friendly Canadian pilots she slipped into the Atlantic from a little-used tributary. After more pillaging, she reentered Wilmington harbor and was decommissioned. She was recommissioned the CSS *Olustee*, made a brief foray into the Atlantic, and was then made into a blockade-runner.

The cruise of the CSS *Shenandoah* was the final chapter in the story of the Confederate commerce raiders. Commissioned in October 1864, she followed in the footsteps of the *Alabama*, lost in June, the *Florida*, lost that same month, and the *Tallahassee*, decommissioned after her spectacular cruise along the northeastern coast of the United States. Her captain, James Waddell, took her on a cruise along the South Atlantic to Cape Horn and into the Indian Ocean. In January 1865 he stopped in Melbourne, Australia, to rest and refit. After several weeks, he continued to hunt for U.S. flag vessels in the north Atlantic, at one point coming within miles of the Arctic Circle. Waddell pillaged the Pacific whaling trade. On June 28, 1865, more than two months after Lee's surrender at Appomattox, Waddell took eleven vessels, sinking them all. Waddell seized a steamer with newspapers on board, somewhat out of date, which told of the fall of Richmond and Jefferson Davis' vow to fight on. Within a month, however, he hailed a British merchantman and was told the truth of the collapse of the Confederacy. Waddell dismounted his guns and sailed around the Cape of Good Hope to Liverpool, England, where he surrendered the *Shenandoah* to the Royal Navy on November 5, 1865. The last Confederate had surrendered.

One unique vessel should be noted. A Danish vessel, the *Staerkodder*, was an ironclad ram sloop of fourteen hundred tons (1271t) with a 300-pounder (136kg) rifle at her bow and two 5-inch (12.7cm) rifles. The

*The CSS **Stonewall**, one of the ironclads built secretly in France and then embargoed by the French government. After the war, she was turned over to the U.S. government, which sold her to Japan.*

Danes, recent losers in the Schlesweig-Holstein War against Prussia, needed to sell the ship, and found a willing buyer in Confederate agent Bulloch. In January 1865, she left port with a Danish crew and was transferred to the Confederate navy on the high seas. Her captain was Thomas Jefferson Page, and she was commissioned the CSS *Stonewall*. But the new, unwieldy ship needed repairs, so Page put in at the Spanish port of La Coruna. Within days, word got out and two U.S. warships, the USS *Niagara* and the USS *Sacramento*, appeared in the bay.

Page was not concerned. The *Stonewall* was an ironclad ram and the *Niagara* and the *Sacramento* were both wooden. When he was ready to go out, he would be glad to take both ships on. In March, the *Stonewall* made several forays toward the two wooden ships, but they declined to stand and fight. In late March, Page, now ordered by the Spanish government to leave the port, fired up the *Stonewall*'s boilers and went to do battle. All day, Page steamed back and forth waiting for the two warships to attack, but neither did. The commander of the *Niagara*, Thomas Craven, feared the loss of both ships if he attacked the ironclad ram. Finally, at nightfall, Page steamed off for the South Atlantic and Nassau. Arriving at Nassau on May 6, Page discovered the surrender of the Confederate government. He sailed the *Stonewall* into Havana and sold her to the Governor-General of Cuba for $16,000, without once having tested her in battle.

BATTLE OF MOBILE BAY

By the late summer of 1864, only three Confederate ports remained unconquered: Mobile Bay, Charleston, and Wilmington. Grant, now commander of all Union ground forces, was of the opinion that a victory at Mobile Bay would allow the Northern forces to slice off several more states from the Confederacy and join with Sherman's campaign in Georgia. Farragut was ordered from New York to make the attack.

A complicating factor was the presence of the ironclad ram CSS *Tennessee* being built in Mobile. Welles feared that the *Tennessee*, commanded by Buchanan, recovered after his wounds aboard the *Merrimack*, would leave the bay and strike at the wooden fleet in blockade. But that was not Buchanan's plan. He knew, as did everyone, that an attack on Mobile Bay was imminent, and his job was to defeat the Union Navy when it came. Buchanan had help in the form of submerged mines, multiple piling lines, a narrow channel, and sunken hulks.

Farragut ordered four of the latest Monitor-class ships sent to him. By July, the USS *Tecumseh*, the USS *Manhattan*, the USS *Chickasaw*, and the USS *Winnebago* were on their way to Farragut. The *Tecumseh* and the *Manhattan* were improved Canonicus-class monitors, each carrying two 15-inch (38.1cm) guns and eleven inches (27.9cm) of armor.

ABOVE: Admiral Farragut's letter home just before the Battle of Mobile Bay. "I am going into Mobile Bay in the morning if 'God is my leader,' as I hope he is." RIGHT: The Confederate ram CSS Tennessee and Farragut's flagship, the USS Hartford, engage at close quarters in Mobile Bay, Alabama. Painting by Tom W. Freeman.

A contemporary engraving of the action in Mobile Bay.

The *Chickasaw* and the *Winnebago* were new four-screw, twin-turret Milwaukee-class monitors, each carrying four 11-inch (27.9cm) guns, two in each turret, and eight inches (20.3cm) of armor. In addition, Farragut had fourteen more men-of-war, including side-wheel gunboats and rigged ships.

At the crack of dawn on April 5, 1864, the Union fleet started into Mobile Bay. The four monitors, led by the *Tecumseh*, were in the starboard column. The remaining fourteen wooden ships, lashed together in pairs, made up the port column. Almost as soon as they entered the bay, the *Tecumseh* veered to port, struck a mine, and went down immediately, with the loss of all but eight hands. Terror

struck, and the captain of the *Brooklyn,* fearing she was among the mines, began backing to avoid them. Farragut, lashed to the rigging of the *Hartford*, his flagship, saw the *Brooklyn*'s movement and knew that unless something was done, his whole fleet would come to a halt directly under the Confederate guns. Farragut uttered the now-famous command, "Damn the torpedoes! Full speed ahead!" The Union fleet steamed forward. Several officers aboard other ships reported hearing their vessels pass over the mines and hearing the firing mechanisms snap shut; but the mines failed to detonate.

As the fleet passed Fort Morgan, the fort's batteries cut into the wooden ships.

Raking fire from the Confederate naval vessels, including the *Tennessee* and the *Selma*, could not be answered because of the angle. As the column passed the forts, the weakest vessels in the rear were cut to pieces by the fort's guns. The *Hartford* cut out across the mined area and was followed by the others in column.

The monitors steered immediately toward the *Tennessee*. The Confederate gunboats accompanying the ram pulled away and headed for the shallows, knowing they were no match for the monitors or the heavy gunboats. There then occurred a lull in the battle as each side took stock of its position and regrouped. Aboard the *Tennessee*, Buchanan ordered the crew to breakfast, but continued a two-knot (1.3m/sec) crawl toward the Union fleet.

When lookouts saw the oncoming *Tennessee*, the fleet went to her. Farragut ordered all ships to attempt to ram the Confederate ironclad. The big wooden frigates began firing on the ironclad, but caused no damage at all. The *Brooklyn* missed in her ramming attempt and was shot up by the *Tennessee*. Next, the *Monongahela* with the *Kennebec* lashed to her side rammed into the ironclad. Other than spinning the *Tennessee* around, the blow did nothing. Once again the *Tennessee*'s gunners blew holes through the wooden ships. Suddenly, the monitor *Manhattan* appeared and fired a 15-inch (38.1cm) solid shot weighing 350 pounds (158.9kg) that completely pierced the *Tennessee*'s iron siding. Immediately, the *Lackawanna* steamed in to ram the ironclad, but missed. Following shots from the *Lackawanna* severed the *Tennessee*'s steering chains on the quarterdeck, and she lost steerage. The *Hartford* then made a run at her, but also missed and was gored by the *Lackawanna* after passing the Hartford. The monitor *Chickasaw*, meanwhile, fired rounds into her continuously.

Finally, Commander James Johnston, the *Tennessee*'s captain, conferred with Buchanan, whose leg was broken. Buchanan ordered Johnston to haul down the colors in order to prevent further bloodshed.

By late morning, the Battle of Mobile Bay was over. Farragut's armada had suffered over 325 casualties against the Confederates' thirty-two. Within days, the forts capitulated to the combined power of the gunboats and Union infantry. The Gulf of Mexico was now completely in Union hands.

WILMINGTON, NORTH CAROLINA: THE FINAL FORT

Only one location kept supplies open to the Confederacy. After the fall of Mobile, Fort Fisher, at Wilmington, remained alone in defiance of the Union blockade. As long as she stood, blockade-runners had a safe haven to enter and deposit their goods. By late 1864, Welles had decided to reduce Fort Fisher, and had appointed David Porter to command the expedition. But Porter knew that Fort Fisher could not be taken by naval action alone, and he implored Grant to provide infantry to make the final combined assault. Grant finally sent Major General Ben Butler with sixty-five hundred men under Godfrey Weitzel.

Butler had a plan that involved the detonation of a large explosive to shock the fort's inhabitants, followed by a land assault by infantry. Porter, always willing to try something new, agreed and provided an old ship, the *Louisiana*, filled with more than two hundred tons (181.6t) of powder. On Christmas Day, 1864, the *Louisiana* was pushed to within a half mile (0.8km) of the fort and, in the dark hours of the morning, exploded. The effect was less than spectacular. Undisturbed inside Fort Fisher, the Confederates thought that a Union gunboat

TOP: The battered CSS Tennessee, *her smokestack gone, surrenders to Farragut's naval forces in Mobile Bay. ABOVE: The* Tennessee, *shown here after her capture in Mobile Bay and her recommissioning as a Union ship.*

The Federal fleet bombarding Fort Fisher, south of Wilmington, North Carolina. After a later assault, it was discovered that the bombardment had had little effect.

had hit a mine and blown up. The plan called for the infantry to be landed on the beach and immediately assault the fort while the navy provided gunfire support. But by noon, no troops had landed on the beach. Porter had his ships open fire.

Within several hours, Weitzel, with the navy's assistance, had twenty-five hundred men, about one-third of his force, on the beach five miles (8km) from the fort. After a reconnaissance, Weitzel knew that his small

force could not possibly take the fort, which, for all the bombardment, was relatively undamaged. Butler had queried Porter on the possibility of the navy steaming into the Cape Fear River and taking the fort from the rear. A reconnaissance showed that this was not possible either. Butler ordered the troops back aboard the transports and headed back to Hampton Roads. Amazingly, he left six hundred infantrymen behind, stranded on the beach in enemy territory. It took two

days, but Porter eventually managed to remove the men safely.

Butler was sacked for the fiasco, and Grant reassured Porter that Fort Fisher would be a primary target. Within two weeks, Grant sent eight thousand troops under General Alfred Terry, with "do or die" orders, to Porter. On January 13, the bombardment opened and, presaging the combined operations of World War II to come eighty years later, more than two hundred boats filled with infantry headed for the shore. Within four hours, all eight thousand troops were ashore and entrenched. The naval bombardment continued for another two days.

Porter, anxious to be involved in every single fray, formed a naval landing party made up of two thousand sailors and marines. This naval landing party would assault the fort from the opposite side at 3:00 P.M. on January 15, when the official assault was to begin. With the signal, the men of the naval landing party began their assault. They were closer than the infantrymen, and the fort's defenders thought they were the main attack. In the open, running down a beach with no fire support and only small arms, the naval party was cut to pieces, with more than three hundred men killed.

The naval assault may have helped. Within minutes, the infantry dashed against the fort from the opposite side. Too close for naval gunfire support or the use of cannons inside the fort, the battle was waged hand-to-hand. Finally, at 9:00 P.M., Terry sent a signal rocket up from the fort announcing the fort's surrender and its occupation. The Union blockade of the South was now complete. From this time on, nothing would come into or out of the South by water.

ABOVE: Every gunner's desire: dismounting the enemy's guns. Once guns were dismounted, they were out of action until after the battle. They were too heavy to remount without considerable equipment and manpower. BELOW: At 3:00 P.M. on January 15, 1864, a naval landing party of two thousand sailors stormed over this open beach to assault Fort Fisher. With no fire support and only small arms, they were easily repelled, and more than three hundred men were killed. Another assault by the infantry and marines at a different location succeeded, and the fort was captured six hours later. This photograph, taken shortly after the battle, shows round shot scattered on the beach.

chapter 6

CONCLUSION

"It's time to blow out the lights aboard. Hoping soon to be with the 'loved ones at home' and my darling wife, I am your very affectionate husband, Symmes."

—Letter from Symmes Browne, Acting Ensign aboard the USS Forest Rose, to his wife, Fannie, May 24, 1864

UNION NAVAL SUCCESSES

With all her ports blockaded and her navy in ruins except for the odd raider at sea, the Confederacy lost the ability to supply, and thus defend, herself. During the four years between 1861 and 1865, the Union Navy's might expanded tremendously. Swifter ships with more powerful guns were being produced. In 1861 the United States was at best a second-rate force on the high seas; by the war's end, it had become the world's foremost naval power. At Mobile Bay in 1864, Farragut had at his command the most powerful naval battery on earth. But, as has usually happened in peacetime, the U.S. Navy was allowed to decline in power during the years between the Civil War and the turn of the century. However, the Spanish-American War and foreign expansion once again spurred growth.

The Union's most remarkable feat during the war was the building of the largest navy in the world from scratch. This buildup was not a slow, methodical pursuit of more modern naval craft, but a sudden, rapid technological expansion involving the construction of modern, multipurpose naval craft suitable for the wide variety of missions that were thrown on the navy by the war government. This modern fleet successfully blockaded more than three thousand miles (4,800km) of coastline, including large ports; defeated every Southern warship; attacked and destroyed Southern coastal forts; gained control of all major rivers and tributaries; and supported the land operations of the Union army.

This success was due in large part to an unusual willingness to experiment with new naval technology. From a wood and steam

navy in 1861, the Union, within four years, effectively produced modern steel warships carrying the largest naval ordnance produced and capable of going head to head with any known warship on earth.

Welles showed remarkable insight in his use of naval officers and their promotion. The old navy was steeped in tradition, particularly where the promotion of officers was concerned. Welles, knowing that his war situation did not allow for the niceties of the old navy's promotion system, promoted and used commanders he knew could get the job done. Admiral David Porter, a loudmouthed firebrand who should have been court-martialed and drummed from the service under the naval etiquette of the times, was instead promoted and used extensively by Welles, who knew he was a very able commander and got results regardless of his personality. Welles also used a junior flag officer, David Farragut, when other, more senior officers were available. Welles knew that Farragut would complete his missions.

UNION NAVAL FAILURES

Despite its tremendous successes, the Union Navy also had its share of shortcomings and failures. As the Union Army did on several occasions, the Union Navy failed to adequately follow up on its coastal victories at Hatteras,

A rare photograph of the building of the ironclad USS **Indianola***. She was later captured by Confederate forces, but was of little use to them since they had to destroy her a month later to prevent her recapture.*

Port Royal, Pensacola, and New Orleans by not having a sufficient infantry force available to press the victory inland.

Farragut and the other commanders suffered from a belief that nothing could withstand the powerful guns that a fleet could bring to bear; some called it "bombardment fever." Yet, they ultimately did come to realize that while the navy could perform certain siege and reduction tasks, it could not achieve major military objectives alone.

Welles suffered from his own fever: "iron fever." He initially believed that the ironclad was the answer to all of his naval problems, without giving adequate consideration to additional factors such as naval firepower, adequate support from ground forces, and deepwater operations.

Whether or not the blockade was truly effective is open to question. There is a historical perspective that holds that the

Southern ports should have been bombarded and captured through combined naval and ground operations. The blockade was extremely costly in terms of men and ships. Yet, statistically, the main objective of the blockade, stopping blockade-runners, was not achieved. Until 1864, the chances of a blockade-runner being captured were less than one in four. Until mid-1864 the blockade was only marginally effective in terms of economic impact on the South. And by the time it became truly effective, the land war had progressed to the point that the outcome was no longer in doubt.

In spite of the successes of the combined operations conducted during the war (e.g. Vicksburg, Wilmington), the primary focus of the Union was on land warfare. Halleck, and later Grant, being army men, felt that the true objective of the war was meeting the enemy on the battlefield and defeating his army. This, of course, was at odds with Scott's plan for the economic strangulation of the South. Perhaps some of the blame for this can be laid on President Lincoln, who felt that the early inaction of his land forces was cause for great concern.

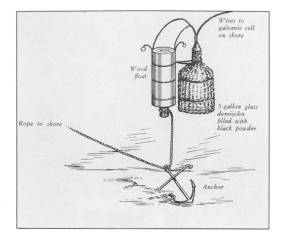

PAGES 118–119: William R. McGrath's painting of the Confederate ironclad CSS Albemarle *engaging Union warships near Plymouth, North Carolina, on April 19, 1864. In this engagement, the* Albemarle *sank the USS* Southfield. *Six months later, in October 1864, she was sunk in the Roanoke River by a daring raiding party of Federal naval commandos.* ABOVE: *An illustration of a naval mine of the type used by Zere McDaniel, Confederate naval saboteur, to sink the USS* Cairo. *It was a wicker-covered glass demijohn, filled with gunpowder and fired by a friction primer. This illustration wrongly assumes an electrical detonating device.* RIGHT: *A contemporary engraving of Confederate naval officers.*

CONFEDERATE NAVAL SUCCESSES

The South was incredibly fortunate to have Stephen Mallory, a true visionary, available to be its Secretary of the Navy. Like the Union command, Mallory was asked to start from scratch and build a formidable fighting force complete with equipment, personnel, lines of supply, lines of communication, arsenals, docks, yards, and ships. The precise extent to which he succeeded is subject to debate, but he was without question far more successful than might reasonably have been expected.

The Confederate Navy employed a half-dozen or so spar torpedo boats, or "Davids," so called for the first one, named CSS **David***. These were semi-submersible boats that sank their targets with a spar torpedo (a long rod with an explosive charge at the end) extending from the bow, then backed off and moved away. They were not very safe, and several of them drowned their crews.*

Prior to the Civil War, the South was a primarily agrarian economy with very little industry. When the war came, the South began a rapid industrialization to the degree allowed by the materials it had available. This industrialization allowed for the construction of an ironclad navy with capable armaments.

The South's lack of an established navy was in some ways a blessing from a technological standpoint. With a severe lack of equipment and technology, individual efforts at technological innovation were encouraged and rewarded. As a result, the Confederacy was the first nation to build and use underwater mines, the first to build an ironclad

warship, and the first to build and use a successful submarine.

CONFEDERATE NAVAL FAILURES

Secretary Stephen Mallory's reliance on large, costly ironclad warships for attack and defense purposes was not successful under the circumstances of limited time, money, and materials. Federal ironclad and wooden-hulled ships were equally vulnerable to ramming. In retrospect, it seems clear that a fleet of fast, cheap Ellet-type rams might have been more effective in the long run.

Mallory's reliance on the expensive commerce raider fleet provided a great deal of publicity, but in the end was not very useful to the South, since the raiders could not bring their prizes into southern ports and benefit the South economically. Mallory's hope that the raiders would draw off major portions of the Union fleet was not fulfilled. Welles assigned some ships to chase the raiders, but this effort was designed mostly to quiet the criticism he received from the civilian mercantile class.

The South failed miserably to exploit its technological advantages. It failed to coordinate and devote the resources necessary for an aggressive mine-laying program in southern

ABOVE: Two Confederate ironclads of the James River Flotilla, CSS Fredericksburg and CSS Virginia II, though built late in the war, saw repeated action in the defense of Richmond, Virginia. Both were blown up to prevent capture after the evacuation of Richmond. RIGHT: Sailors and marines aboard the USS Miami open fire on the CSS Albemarle as she rams and sinks the USS Southfield at Plymouth, North Carolina, on April 19, 1864. Both paintings by Tom W. Freeman.

harbors and rivers. Mines were developed, built, and emplaced by engineers like Zere McDaniel, Matthew Fontaine Maury, and others on an *ad hoc* basis. Experiments with small, fast, shallow-draft boats armed with explosive torpedoes on spars proved them very effective. Yet none of this innovation was coordinated at any level; the inventors were simply left to ply their respective efforts wherever they felt they would do the most good.

NAVAL INNOVATION

If anything can be said of the American Civil War, it is that it allowed individual initiative to be brought to the fore. Naval warfare was completely revolutionized. Iron ships replaced wooden ships forever. Muzzle loading, smoothbore cannon disappeared in favor of more powerful and accurate breech-loading rifled cannon. Faster, more powerful steam engines were developed, not to be replaced until gasoline, diesel, and eventually nuclear power replaced coal.

Most importantly, the army and the navy found that, through cooperation, the tactical advantages of each could be combined to make an imposing assault force. With the navy's ability to bring large-caliber weapons to bear and the infantry's ability to maneuver on land, no fort was safe. The lessons learned at Fort Henry, Fort Donelson, Shiloh, Vicksburg, Hatteras, and Fort Fisher would well serve men later landing at Normandy, Iwo Jima, and Inchon.

TOM FREEMAN
© 1993

BIBLIOGRAPHY

Bearss, Edwin C. *Hardluck Ironclad*. Baton Rouge, La.: Louisiana State University Press, l966.

Beers, Henry Putney. *Guide to the Archives of the Government of the Confederate States of America*. Washington, D.C.: National Archives and Records Service, l968. (NARS Pub. 68-15).

Beers, Henry Putney, and Kenneth W. Munden. *Guide to the Federal Archives Relating to the Civil War*. Washington, D.C.: National Archives and Records Service, l962. (NARS Pub. 63-1).

Boatner, Mark M. III. *The Civil War Dictionary,* rev. ed. New York: David MacKay Co., 1988.

Canney, Donald L. *The Old Steam Navy*. 2 vols. Annapolis: The Naval Institute Press, 1990.

Coggins, Jack. *Arms and Equipment of the Civil War*. New York: The Fairfax Press, 1983.

Evans, Clement A., ed. *Confederate Military History*. 13 vols. rpt. Secaucus, NJ: Blue & Grey Press, n.d.

Gibbons, Tony. *Warships and Naval Battles of the Civil War*. New York: W. H. Smith Publishers, Inc., 1989.

Hewitt, Lawrence L. *Port Hudson: Confederate Bastion on the Mississippi*. Baton Rouge, La.: Louisiana State University Press, 1987.

Horan, James D. *Confederate Agent*. New York: Crown Publishers, 1956.

Johnson, Robert U., and Clarence C. Buel. *Battles and Leaders of the Civil War*. 4 vols. New York: The Century Co., 1887.

Jones, Virgil Carrington. *The Civil War at Sea*. 3 vols. New York: Holt, Rinehart & Winston, 1961.

Lord, Francis A. *Civil War Collector's Encyclopedia*. Secaucus, New Jersey: Castle, 1982.

Lucas, Daniel B. *Memoir of John Yates Beall*. Montreal, Que.: John Lovell, 1865.

Mahan, Alfred Thayer. *Gulf and Inland Waters*. New York: Chas. Scribner's Sons, 1883.

Manucy, Albert. *Artillery Through the Ages*. Washington, D.C.: Government Printing Office, 1949.

Maury, Richard L. *A Brief Sketch of the Work of Matthew Fontaine Maury*. Richmond, Va.: Whittet & Shepperson, l915

Miller, Francis T., ed. *The Photographic History of the Civil War*. 10 vols. New York: The Review of Reviews, 1912.

Milligan, John D., ed. *From the Fresh Water navy: 1861–64*. Naval Letter Series: Volume Three. Annapolis, Md.: Naval Institute Press, 1970.

Nash, Howard P. *A Naval History of the Civil War*. New York: A. S. Barnes, Co., 1972.

Perry, Milton F. *Infernal Machines: The Story of Confederate Submarine and Mine Warfare*. Baton Rouge, La.: Louisiana State University Press, 1965.

Porter, David D. *Naval History of the Civil War* rpt. Secaucus, N.J.: Castle, 1984.

Ripley, Warren. *Artillery and Ammunition of the Civil War*. 4th ed. Charleston, S.C.: The Battery Press, 1984.

Scharf, J. Thomas. *History of the Confederate States Navy*. Baltimore, 1887. rpt. New York: The Fairfax Press, 1977.

Silverstone, Paul H. *Warships of the Civil War Navies*. Annapolis, Md.: The Naval Institute Press, 1989.

Stern, Philip Van Dorn. *Secret Missions of the Civil War*. New York: Rand McNally, 1959.

U.S. Department of the Interior. National Park Service. *The Story of a Civil War Gunboat: USS* Cairo. Washington, D.C.: Government Printing Office, 1971.

U.S. War Department. *The War of the Rebellion. Official Records of the Union and Confederate Armies*. 73 vols. Washington, D.C.: Government Printing Office, 1880–1901.

————. *The War of the Rebellion. Official Records of the Union and Confederate Navies*. 31 vols. Washington, D.C.: Government Printing Office, 1895–1929.

————. *The Ordnance Manual for use by the Officers of the United States Army*. 3rd ed. Philadelphia: J. P. Lippincott & Co, 1862.

Wideman, John. *The Sinking of the USS* Cairo. Jackson, Miss.: University Press of Mississippi, 1992.

PHOTO CREDITS

Brown Brothers: pp. 11 inset, 12 right, 14 left, 23, 35 top, 38 right, 40, 55 left, 59, 68 right, 79, 81 top, 95 left, 103 right, 109 top, 110

Corbis-Bettmann: pp. 14 right, 24, 33 right, 34, 36, 37 left, 38 bottom, 41 top, 43, 53, 56 bottom, 61 top, 63 inset, 65 bottom, 67, 71, 77, 78, 83 inset, 84 right, 91 right, 94 bottom, 97 inset, 104, 105 left, 108, 113 inset, 117 left, 120 right

©Tom W. Freeman, Courtesy of SM&S Naval Prints, Inc., Forest Hill, MD: pp. 1, 2-3, 52, 64, 70, 86, 88, 92, 93, 102-103, 106-107, 114-115, 122 left, 122-123

Frank Leslie's Illustrated Newspaper: pp. 10-11, 28-29, 44-45, 58-59, 62-63, 82-83, 96-97, 112-113

Library of Congress: front endpaper; pp. 15, 16, 25, 33 left, 41 bottom, 46, 47 right, 48 center, 49, 60, 66, 72 left, 80, 81 bottom, 84 left, 87, 89 both, 95 right, 109 bottom, 111 bottom, 116

Painting by William R. McGrath, Courtesy WRM Graphics, Inc., Cleveland, OH: pp. 6-7, 19, 20-21, 26-27, 74-75, 90-91, 98-99, 118-119

National Archives: back endpaper; pp. 18, 32, 35 bottom, 42, 47 left, 48 right, 100, 105 right, 111 top, 117 right, 121

North Wind Picture Archives: pp. 9, 13, 17, 21 right, 29 inset, 31, 37 right, 38 left, 50, 51, 54, 55 right, 56 top, 61 bottom, 65 top, 68 left, 69, 85 both, 94 top, 101, 106 left

Superstock: pp. 30, 45 inset, 48 left, 72-73

Don Troiani, Southbury, CT: p. 12 left

Painting by Don Troiani, Southbury, CT: p. 39

U.S. Government Printing Office: p. 57; copy photography by Christopher Bain: p. 120 left

Front Jacket Illustration: ©Tom W. Freeman, Courtesy of SM&S Naval Prints, Inc., Forest Hill, MD

Back Jacket Photograph: Corbis-Bettmann

INDEX